Getting Together

Getting Together,

Building a Relationship That Gets to YES

by
Roger Fisher
and
Scott Brown
of the Harvard Negotiation Project

Houghton Mifflin Company
Boston • 1988

Library of Congress Cataloging-in-Publication Data

Fisher, Roger, date.
  Getting together.

  1. Negotiation.   2. Interpersonal relations.
I. Brown, Scott.   II. Title.
BF637.N4F58   1988   158'.5   88-747
ISBN 0-395-47099-4

Printed in the United States of America

Q 10 9 8 7 6 5 4 3 2 1

Research at Harvard University is undertaken with the expectation of publication. In such publication, the authors alone are responsible for statements of fact, opinions, recommendations, and conclusions expressed. Publication in no way implies approval or endorsement by Harvard University, any of its faculties, or by the President and Fellows of Harvard College.

TO

CAROLINE FISHER

Carrie, Scott has generously agreed that
this book be dedicated to you, on the
fortieth anniversary of a working
relationship that keeps working
better and better

Acknowledgments

This book began with our concern for U.S.-Soviet relations and with our belief that the real problem in our relationship lies not in the technical issues of arms control or military hardware, but in how our two countries deal with each other and with their differences. As we thought about what help we might be able to offer governmental leaders, we realized that clear thinking about relationship issues could be more general, more powerful, and more persuasive if it drew not only from international relations, but from personal and business relations as well. This approach caused us to draw on the experience, judgment, and ideas of a great many others.

Without mercy we have picked the brains of friends and family, staff and students, writers and readers, professionals and lay people of all kinds. Each has helped us develop and refine our ideas, sometimes as part of a joint experiment, and often unknowingly. We are grateful to all. Thank you. We hope that in exploring how to build relationships we have not ruined any.

Over the past few years, Carol Gilligan and Victor Kremenyuk have been particularly helpful in illuminating for us how differently people see things. We want to thank our editors and supporters at Houghton Mifflin, who encouraged us along the way and put up with our delays. In particular, thanks to Robie Macauley, who guided us in the early stages of the manuscript, and to Luise Erdmann, whose sharp pencil saved the reader from many wordy sentences and repetitive discourse.

Special thanks go to the Carnegie Corporation of New York, whose ongoing support made this book possible. Fritz Mosher and Deana Arsenian have given us support when we needed it, but have let us pursue our sometimes tortuous path without interference or pressure.

Our families and friends have played a crucial role. Caroline Fisher, Francis Fisher, and Mary Kendall have given generously of their time, their criticisms, their suggestions, and their unflagging moral support. From them, we received the kind of detailed feedback that helped us clarify not only what we said but what we thought.

Finally, from all our professional colleagues in and around the Harvard Negotiation Project we have received the kind of intellectual challenge, cooperation, and support that has made the Project such an exhilarating and productive place to work. Francine Pillemer and Michael Keane were particularly helpful in forcing us to appreciate the important role emotions play in a good working relationship. Bruce Allyn, whether in Moscow or Cambridge, helped us understand Soviet perceptions. Wayne Davis, who would never accept a fuzzy concept or blurry statement, worked as hard as we to sharpen every idea. Finally, Bruce Patton not only helped us brainstorm, reorganize, and edit every chapter and every thought but took on other tasks that made it possible for us to keep working on the book.

ROGER FISHER
SCOTT BROWN

Contents

ix

Introduction

Whether we are young or old, rich or poor, American, Brazilian, or Russian, we all have relationships that are important to us. Even Robinson Crusoe had his man Friday. It is through our relations with others that we work and play, earn a living, build a family, cope with problems, and enjoy life. Not only infants depend on others. We all do.

The world does not start afresh every morning. Each day we deal with people we have met before and will meet again. We complain to the landlord, listen to the boss, handle a customer, smooth out a family quarrel, or visit a friend. In almost every case, the fact that the relationship is continuing affects the outcome of the encounter. Stripped of our ongoing relationships, we would have no family, no friends, no colleagues, no employees, no supervisors, no government, no customers, and no one to write us a letter or meet us for lunch.

Some relationships work better than others. We all know people with whom we feel comfortable, secure, able to talk through a problem, and confident. With others we feel uncomfortable, frustrated, and mistrustful. We rarely understand why some relationships work well and others don't. We tend to accept the quality of a relationship as inevitable: "That's the way it is. We just don't get along." We blame problems on the other person and assume that there is little we can do to improve the way we interact.

Although it takes two to have a relationship, it takes only one to change its quality. Just as we react to others, they react to us. By changing our behavior, we will change the way they react. This book is based on the premise that change is possible and that each of us can improve the way we deal with others.

There is, however, no way that each of us can produce relationships that allow us to sail through life in perfect harmony, happily and efficiently resolving all differences. In this often harsh world there are circumstances we cannot control. There are even limits on the extent to which we can control ourselves. But we do make choices. We can make a difference. Given these constraints, what is the best advice that clear thinking and organized common sense can offer?

Poor choices: three dilemmas

As we try to build a relationship *and* deal with immediate problems, our assumptions sometimes compel us to choose between unattractive options. We may find ourselves asking such questions as:

What is the best way to avoid disagreement? Should I give in or sweep a problem under the rug?

(Assumption: Avoiding disagreement is a good goal for a relationship.)

Should I risk the relationship to get what I want, or should I sacrifice my interests for the sake of the relationship?

(Assumption: There is a tradeoff between substantive interests and a good relationship.)

Should I take the first step to improve the relationship, hoping the other person will reciprocate, or should I wait and see what he does and respond accordingly?

(Assumption: Reciprocity of some kind is a good guideline for how to treat people.)

The purpose of this book is to present better assumptions, better choices, and better answers. It continues a long-term concern for helping people deal with their shared and conflicting interests. A previous book, *Getting to YES: Negotiating Agreement Without Giving In* (Houghton Mifflin, 1981), focused on the negotiation of particular transactions. We all know, however, that the outcome of a particular transaction depends not only on our negotiation skills. It also depends on our relationship with those with whom we are negotiating. This book will articulate some basic concepts that should help people establish and maintain the kind of relationship they need to get what they want.

Pursue a "working" relationship

At the outset, we need to clarify what we mean by a "good" relationship. What each of us wants from a relationship varies greatly. But whether I hope through my relationship with you to gain love, money, security, or something else, we are bound to face conflicting interests, perceptions, and values. Differences are bound to arise. And we will not get what we want unless we can handle those differences. In each of our relationships, whether between individuals, businesses, religious groups, or governments, we should seek to establish and maintain those qualities that will make it a good "working" relationship — one that is able to deal well with differences. The proposition that this should be a goal for every relationship is discussed in Chapter 1.

Separate the people from the problem

The severity of the differences between two individuals, or between two governments, tends to affect the way they interact. Unfortunately, when the differences are especially serious, such as those between the United States and the Soviet Union, the relationship tends to be especially poor and unable to handle them. If we want a relationship that can deal with serious differences, we have to improve the process itself, independent of the particular substantive problems involved.

Relationship issues concern the way we deal with people: clearly or ambiguously, honestly or deceptively, logically or emotionally, and so forth. Substantive issues are those that might typically be included in an agreement — such matters as money, dates, time, property, terms, and conditions. It seems best to work on the process of a relationship — *how* we deal with each other — independent of all substantive differences. Deal with both sets of problems, people problems and substantive ones, but do not link them. This proposition is developed in Chapter 2.

Be unconditionally constructive

On the premise that a valuable goal is a working relationship, and that relationship issues can usefully be separated from substantive ones, Chapter 3 outlines a suggested method or strategy for building a problem-solving relationship. The method neither counts on others to follow our example nor does it have us follow theirs. The advice, rather, is to be "unconditionally constructive." This means that in a relationship with you, I should do those things and only those things that are both good for the relationship and good for me — whether or not you reciprocate.

The balance of the book elaborates on this method, explaining how it applies to each of the qualities needed in a good working relationship.

Each relationship is unique. But the basic qualities that make it possible for any relationship to deal easily and well with differences are not. The method of being unconditionally constructive in a relationship can be applied by governments, businesses, and individuals. It can help start a new relationship or improve an old one. And, although these guidelines may be more relevant to a long-term relationship, they also apply to a one-time negotiation between strangers, where the relationship established in the first minute may well determine what kind of deal, if any, will be reached within the hour.

Unless you are alone on a desert island, the method described in these few pages should help you achieve whatever it is that you want.

Getting Together

I | An
Overview

1 | The Goal

A relationship that can deal well with differences

WE ALL FIND it easier to deal with some people than with others. In this sense, we may know a good relationship when we see one, but may fail to understand the qualities that make it good. The less clearly we understand what our goal is, the more difficult it will be to attain.

What we want and what we need in a relationship are unclear

Our assumptions about relationships are often inconsistent with the kind of relationship we need to get what we want. These inconsistencies lead to confusion about our objective.

We use the words "relations" and "relationship" in many ways. In one sense, "relations" are those to whom we are related by blood or marriage. In another sense, "relations" refer to the state of affairs between two countries. When a couple speaks of "having a relationship," they may mean that they are living together. A banker may say that his bank has "a special relationship" with a client, yet even colleagues will have widely divergent views of just what

3

that means. From a dozen officers at the same bank we received definitions of a "good" relationship as diverse as:

"A long-standing pattern of doing business."
"We have made a lot of money dealing with them."
"Great financial potential."
"Our president plays golf with the chairman of their board."
"They pay their bills; we can trust them."
"We have to do things for them in return for past favors."

Some businesses do try to characterize their relationships with clients and customers. One management consulting firm, for example, keeps track of its clients in terms of the length of the relationship, the amount of money at stake, the number of people involved on each side, and the frequency and extent of communication. But even a rough effort to define a business relationship is rare.

When people describe relations between individuals or among nations in such vague terms as "cold," "formal," or "friendly," they often have no practical definition of a good relationship.

We confuse good relations with approval. One way of expressing strong disapproval of another's conduct is to terminate the relationship: "After what she did, I will never speak to her again!" Such "banishment" is common to personal, business, and diplomatic relations. A company may refuse to do business with another after receiving poor service or feeling cheated. And a government may recall its ambassador and "break diplomatic relations" to express disapproval of another government's behavior. It is therefore not surprising that people frequently assume the reverse, that establishing or maintaining a relationship demonstrates approval of the other's conduct.

But expressing disapproval by disrupting a relationship is

rarely, if ever, a good idea. Refusing to deal with someone will rarely solve an immediate problem; it will almost certainly impair our ability to solve future problems. If I know that circumstances will require my ongoing interaction with another person or institution — whether in the family, in the office, or internationally — then I should continue to deal with them now even if I disapprove of their conduct.

If two nations are caught up in an escalating conflict that may lead to warfare, the last thing they should do is break diplomatic relations, no matter how egregious one believes the other's behavior. The wise parent keeps up a close relationship with a son even when condemning his conduct:

> "Johnny, you know I love you, but you *must* not mark up the wallpaper with your new crayons. I will take them away for this afternoon. Please sit here with me while we talk to make sure that you understand why."

We are confused by the role of shared values. In general, the greater the extent to which you and I share values and perceptions, the fewer differences we will have and the more easily we will find a basis for dealing with them that both of us will consider fair. We may thus tend to equate a good relationship with shared values.

But it would be a mistake to define a good relationship as one in which we agree easily, just as it would be a mistake to define a good road as one that is easy to build. While it is easier to build a good road across a prairie than through mountains, a good road through mountains may be more valuable than one across a prairie. Similarly, a good relationship among parties with sharp differences may be more valuable than one among parties who find it easy to agree.

We see our goal as avoiding disagreement. Many of us are taught as children that it is "naughty" to quarrel. We are led to believe that the "right" kind of relationship is one in which there is no apparent disagreement. Serious as well as small differences are swept under the rug. Partly as a result of such an upbringing, many people feel uncomfortable with conflict of any kind.

The very word "disagreeable" has lost its original meaning of being at variance and has come to mean causing displeasure. People find it disagreeable to disagree. Even family members or close friends, as soon as they become aware of a difference of views, may avoid talking about it. For some, the goal of a good relationship is a make-believe world without differences: "We have a marvelous relationship: we agree on everything."

A particular vision of this kind of relationship is one in which others do what we want. A father might say, "I have an excellent relationship with my son; he does everything I ask and never talks back." Many authoritarian governments, from the Soviet Union to South Korea, believe that a good relationship — with allies or constituents — is one without dissent. Even in the United States, some people apparently believe that our relationship with Honduras, for example, is better than that with France because Honduras follows U.S. policy more often.

No matter how well we think we know what is best for someone else, trying to impose our views on them is more likely to build problems for the future than to build a successful relationship.

Who "we" are is treated as fixed. Once we find ourselves in an adversarial relationship, we tend to think of "them" as someone on "the other side." We exclude the possibility of developing a relationship so effective that there are no longer two opposing sides, but two partners facing the future, side by side.

In courting, we recognize that our goal is to turn an outsider into a member of the family. But in other contexts we are less likely to appreciate the extent of the change that is possible. Building a successful team, whether on the field or in the office, changes the approach to problems. Each member of the team, instead of asking, "What do *I* want? What are *my* interests?" should be asking, "What do *we* want?" and "How do *we* see *our* interests?"

Looking forward to a change of roles goes beyond the professor's advice: "Be nice to your students; someday one may be your boss." It means keeping open the possibility of so changing a relationship that adversaries become partners. Such changes are common in the history of U.S. foreign relations. With each of several former enemies — Great Britain, Canada, Mexico, Spain, Germany, Japan, and China — the United States has now developed a constructive working relationship. While my immediate goal may be improving the way our side deals with your side, my long-term goal may be bringing our sides together.

A good relationship: Having what we need to get what we want

What we *want*: good substantive outcomes. In every relationship, we are likely to want immediate substantive results, such as money, comfort, economic well-being, profit, property, or security. We want the kind of relationship that will best help achieve such interests.

We also *want*: inner peace. After an encounter, we may have an emotional reaction that is as important as the substantive outcome. After a business meeting with one person, we may feel competent, confident, and content — the sort of feelings we echo when we say, "It is always a pleasure to deal with you." After a meeting with someone else, we may feel uneasy, tense, or angry.

Whether we are negotiating with our spouse over where

to go on vacation, with a client over fees, or with the Soviets over arms control, we want a relationship that leaves
us feeling positive. We want peace of mind. We want to be
able to say: "I can work things out with those people." If
we don't feel positive after the last transaction, we may
dread the next and have more difficulty dealing with it.

What we *need*: an ability to deal with differences. We
know that the other party to any relationship also has interests, interests that may differ from ours. And as we try
to deal with our differing interests, we will discover that we
have differing perceptions and values. As time passes and
as we learn more, the interests, perceptions, and values of
both sides are likely to change. These differing wants, perceptions, and values, and the changes in them that take
place over time, provide the endless grist for every
relationship.

Suppose that I want the office to behave like one big
happy family, while my boss wants our relationship to be
strictly business. Or suppose you are interested in a purely
Platonic relationship with a friend who has more intimate
ideas in mind. Or suppose I am looking for a big investment
from a relative who thinks it is a mistake to mix family and
business. Or suppose one country is looking forward to a
live-and-let-live relationship based primarily on trade and
investment, whereas its neighbor would like to use its resources to influence the politics of an entire region. The test
of a good relationship is whether it is able to deal successfully with such differences, including those about the kind
of relationship the parties should have. It is this problem-
solving aspect of a relationship that we call a "working"
relationship.

Competing and changing interests create problems. The
working relationship we need is one that produces a solu-

tion that satisfies the competing interests as well as possible, with little waste, in a way that appears legitimate in the eyes of each of the parties. The solution should also be durable and efficiently reached.

A robust relationship should be able to produce such outcomes in the face of differences in values, perceptions, and interests. It should be able to cope successfully with times when I disapprove of something you did and when we both feel anger rather than affection. It should be strong enough to keep the problem-solving process going even if we develop conflicting views about the relationship itself.

To deal successfully with a difference does not mean that it will disappear. I may want to watch *Masterpiece Theatre* at the very time that you want to watch a Sunday football game; but our relationship should enable us to work out an accommodation that is satisfactory to both of us, whether we flip a coin, take turns, buy another television set, or go bowling.

The ability to deal with differences depends upon a few basic elements

We can measure the health of an individual by checking a few basic elements, such as the blood system, the breathing system, the nervous system, and the digestive system. To measure the health of a relationship, we need to look at the basic qualities that allow it to cope successfully with differences. Six such qualities seem fundamental. Each feature will be discussed in turn, here briefly and at greater length in the chapters that follow.

1. **It helps to balance reason and emotion.** Many aspects of a relationship are not rational. We often react emotionally, not logically, in pursuit of some purpose. Emotions

such as fear, anger, frustration, or even love may disrupt otherwise thoughtful actions. Emotions are normal, necessary, and often essential to problem-solving. They can convey important information, help us marshal our resources, and inspire us to action. Wisdom is seldom found without them. Nonetheless, the ability of two people to deal well with their differences will be greater to the extent that reason and emotion are in some kind of balance.

We cannot work well with another person when emotions overwhelm our reason: we cannot make wise decisions in the middle of a temper tantrum. But neither is logic alone sufficient for solving problems and building a relationship. Rather, we need both reason informed by emotion and emotion guided and tempered by reason. This balance between logic and emotion is a practical definition of working rationality.

2. Understanding helps. If we are going to achieve an outcome that will satisfy the interests of both, at least acceptably, and leave each of us feeling fairly treated, we will need to understand each other's interests, perceptions, and notions of fairness. Unless I have a good idea of what you think the problem is, what you want, why you want it, and what you think might be fair, I will be groping in the dark for an outcome that will meet your interests as well as mine. You, too, will be seriously handicapped unless you understand how I see things. Whether we agree or not, the better we understand each other, the better our chance of creating a solution we can both accept.

3. Good communication helps. Understanding requires effective communication. And even though in general we may understand each other, the quality of a particular outcome and the efficiency with which it is reached are likely to depend on communication about that particular issue. The more effectively we communicate about our differences, the better we will understand each other's concerns and the better our chances for reaching a mutually acceptable agreement. But the manner and extent of our communication do more than improve understanding. The more openly we communicate, the less basis there is for suspicion. We in the United States can feel our distrust of the Soviet Union begin to diminish as it opens its doors to the West. And the more we believe the other side has heard and understood our views, and we theirs, the more likely we will feel that an agreement is fair and balanced. Within reasonable limits, the more communication, the better the working relationship.

4. Being reliable helps. My communicating with you is not worth much if you do not believe me. And commitments that are entered into lightly or disregarded easily are often worse than none. Blind trust will not help me work with others, since misplaced trust will damage a relationship more than healthy skepticism. But well-founded trust, based on honest and reliable conduct over a period of time, can greatly enhance our ability to cope with conflict. The more honest and reliable we are with respect to each other, the better our chance of producing good outcomes.

5. Persuasion is more helpful than coercion. In a particular transaction, you and I may be more interested in the immediate outcome than in our long-term relationship. Each of us will try to affect the other's decisions, and the way in which we do so will have a profound effect on the quality of the relationship. At one extreme, I can try to inspire your voluntary cooperation through education, logical argument, moral persuasion, and my own example. At the other extreme, I can try to coerce you by worsening your alternatives and by warnings, threats, extortion, and physical

force. The more coercive the means of influence, the less
likely it is that the outcome will reflect both of our concerns, and the less legitimate it is likely to be in the eyes of
at least one of us. The less coercive the modes of influence,
the better our ability to work with each other.

6. Mutual acceptance helps. If we are to deal well with our
differences, we need to accept each other as someone
worth dealing with. Feeling accepted, worthy, and valued
is a basic human psychological need. Unless you listen to
my views, accept my right to have views that differ from
yours, and take my interests into account, I am unlikely to
want to deal with you. And if we do not deal with each
other, we will not even begin to resolve our differences.

Acceptance is not an either/or phenomenon but a matter
of degree. The higher the degree of acceptance, the better
the chance of working out differences and producing good
outcomes. Indeed, generally speaking, the more a relationship partakes of each of the qualities outlined above, the
greater the ability of the people in that relationship to solve
their problems wisely and effectively.

Some features are not essential to a good working relationship

If our analysis at the beginning of this chapter about common mistakes is correct, then it is important to note two
qualities that are *not* required in a relationship that deals
well with differences.

Approval. A good working relationship does not require
approval. It should survive situations in which each side
seriously *disapproves* of the other's values, positions, as-
pirations, or conduct. When someone wants to "break" relations with those of whose conduct he disapproves, he

usually does so to send a message and exert pressure toward changing that conduct. We can influence the behavior of others more effectively, however, if we continue to deal with them so that we may understand their interests, make sure they understand ours, and bring to bear upon them our full persuasive powers.

It is possible to convey disapproval by means other than terminating a relationship. At the height of the notoriety of Senator Joseph McCarthy, he was brought as a guest to the Metropolitan Club in Washington, D.C., and introduced to the distinguished lawyer John Lord O'Brian. It is reported that when the senator held out his hand, Mr. O'Brian said, "Senator, as a symbol of my strong disapproval of what you are doing, I would rather not shake your hand. If you would like, I would be happy to come to your office at some time convenient to you and we could discuss our differences."

Lawyers routinely — and rightly — represent clients of whose conduct they disapprove. The better the working relationship between lawyer and client, the better job the lawyer is able to do. And the better the working relationship that the lawyer has with *opposing* counsel, the better the client is served.

In recent years, the United States wisely continued to maintain diplomatic relations with the governments of Afghanistan and Nicaragua despite political differences so strong that in each case the United States was concurrently providing military support to those trying to overthrow the government.

Since the reason for wanting a good working relationship is to resolve differences peacefully and effectively, the more serious the disagreements, the more important it is to have a good way to deal with them. Between the Soviet Union and the United States, differences of ideology and perception, and the vast nuclear weaponry that might be used in any armed conflict, make an effective working relationship important, even if difficult to build. The more dangerous and serious the differences, the more important it is that the two governments have a relationship in which they are able to handle those differences efficiently and with the kind of understanding and honesty that will reduce the risk of disaster.

Shared values. A good working relationship does not require shared values. The more similar our perceptions of the world and our concepts of fairness, the fewer differences we are likely to have and the easier it is likely to be for us to deal with them. If we are selecting individuals with whom to have a relationship, we will want to take shared values into account. But we do not want to confine our problem-solving abilities to those relationships in which the problems are small or easy to resolve.

American businessmen often find it difficult to work and compete with the Japanese because of the countries' different approaches to business and different views of what constitutes appropriate conduct. But, although trade relations between the two countries are filled with serious and emotional disputes, both countries understand that the success of their efforts to reach economic goals and sound trade agreements depends on their ability to work with each other despite differing values.

Knowing the goal is not enough

This chapter has identified the ability to deal well with differences as a goal for every relationship. To achieve our substantive goals, we need effective working relationships, relationships that have a high degree of rationality, understanding, communication, reliability, noncoercive means of influence, and acceptance. Each of those elements is part of the *process* of interaction between two people and independent of their substantive interests. Before exploring a general strategy for improving the process of interaction, we need to separate issues of process from issues of substance.

2 | First Step

Disentangle relationship issues from substantive ones

IT IS EASY to confuse "the relationship" with the substantive interests we want it to serve: "I've got a good relationship with my boss. He gives me a raise every year." "U.S. relations with Japan are getting worse; look at the trade deficit." The relationship process and what it produces often seem indistinguishable.

Think separately about the relationship as a process
In every situation we have two kinds of concerns: the way we handle the situation — process — and the results — substance. Process and substance are distinct but related: one affects the other. Consider, for example, a classroom, where the learning process — lectures, exercises, discussion, and exams — is distinct from the subject of the lessons — geometry, Shakespeare, or chemistry. Yet the way the subject is taught affects what the students learn. If we want to improve the results, we will have to improve the process. The concept of a good educational process, and a strategy for building one, may be the same regardless of whether we are teaching arithmetic, history, or French.

Similarly, in a small business, our immediate concern

may be with manufacturing and marketing good lawn mowers at low cost. But we are almost certain to do it better if we separate issues of the management process, such as how the company makes decisions and how it treats its employees, from issues regarding the kind of lawn mowers it makes and the prices it charges for them. Good management should produce good decisions, but we are unlikely to get good management if we focus only on good lawn mowers. Even the production manager should think about the way he manages people independent of particular decisions about lawn mowers.

To get good results in a relationship, we need to focus both on the results themselves and on the kind of process that will yield those results. We need to ask ourselves what a well-managed relationship looks like and how we can develop one. In a relationship, each of us is a joint manager of the process, a manager with significant if limited ability to shape the relationship and to determine how it functions. Like the production manager, we need to think about how we deal with problems as well as the problems themselves.

If we fail to think separately about the relationship as a process to be managed, we are almost certain to subordinate it to short-term substantive concerns. Each time we deal with someone, we are likely to have our minds on an immediate substantive objective. However important the *way* we deal with each other may be, it often looks less urgent than our immediate goal.

We are likely to focus on the result, not on how to get it. At a restaurant, my mind may be on getting my fettuccine Alfredo quickly, not on understanding the waiter's problems with the kitchen. Even at home, getting the results we want in the day-to-day details of money, meals, clean clothes, and auto repairs may take precedence over thinking about the kind of relationship we would like to have with members of the household. And at the office, this quarter's profit may divert attention from relationships with customers and employees.

In international affairs, urgent problems can similarly divert attention from relationship concerns that are more important. This is true whether it is Soviet officials withholding, for domestic reasons, news of the Chernobyl nuclear disaster from its downwind neighbors or an American president criticizing the Soviet Union in order to appear strong before an election.

Even when we do think about the relationship, we are likely to think about it in terms of results, such as profitability, a customer who comes back, a client who pays bills promptly, or a union that does not strike; we fail to think about the pattern of our interaction and how it might be improved. But if a small business owner fails to think about what makes his relationships work, he may find that he has customers who fade away, clients who pay bills late, and a union that strikes every time its contract expires.

If we think separately about how to establish and maintain a good working relationship, we can deal more easily with matters of substance. One couple may be able to handle an overdrawn checking account as little more than an inconvenience that suggests a need for better coordination, whereas another couple may find that the same issue provokes a heated discussion over fault and blame that prevents them from resolving anything for the future. It is easier to build a working relationship if we pay attention to process as well as substance and pursue each independently and vigorously.

Pursue relationship and substantive goals independently

Even among people who distinguish quite clearly between process and substance and think about each, there is a tendency to trade one off against the other. I may recognize that the less I differ with others, the easier it is to have a good working relationship. This recognition often leads to one of two equally mistaken strategies: either I insist that you agree with me so that we can have a good relationship, or I give in to you on a matter of substance, hoping to improve the relationship. But either way, mixing substance with process damages the ability of the relationship to solve the next problem.

Don't make a relationship contingent on agreement. When we call on another person to concede an issue, we may put it this way:

> Don't make a mountain out of a molehill. Let's not upset our friendship over one issue. Go along with me on this point.

In business and international relations, too, asking for a substantive concession is a common relationship-building strategy. In its relations with North Vietnam, for instance, the United States has said that "it would not improve relations with Hanoi until the missing-in-action question was resolved and until Hanoi withdrew its troops from Cambodia" (*New York Times*, September 4, 1985, p. A8).

Other governments have similarly used the carrot of a better relationship to justify a request for a substantive concession. The Soviet Union has called on the United States to improve relations by stopping the testing of nuclear weapons and by respecting the SALT II arms limitations. The United States, in turn, has told the Soviet Union to improve the relationship by getting out of Afghanistan and by allowing more dissidents to leave the USSR. No

matter how laudable either nation's goal may be, a concession by one to a demand from the other will not improve
the way the two governments are able to deal with their
differences in the future. It is likely to provoke more unilateral demands and less joint problem-solving.

Why do people make this mistake? When a particular
substantive negotiation is about to begin, we are likely to
start with the questions, "What shall *we* do? What is *our*
position?" When we want to improve an ongoing relationship, we are likely to start with the question, "What should
they do to better the relationship?" This pattern reflects a
widely held assumption that improving a relationship is up
to the other side.

It is more useful to reverse the questions. In any substantive negotiation, when we are seeking to influence some decision by the other side, it helps to begin by asking ourselves what decision we would like *the other side* to make
(and then consider what we might do to make that decision
more likely). When the issue is building a relationship,
when we have more control over our own behavior than
over theirs, we should start by asking ourselves what *we*
might do to improve the relationship.

Don't try to buy a better relationship. While many people
believe that they can demand (and achieve) substantive
concessions as a prize for a "good" relationship, others believe that they can "buy" a good relationship by making
substantive concessions. But again, giving in on a current
problem will not help build a process for solving future
problems. A good working relationship is not for sale. And
to make a substantive concession for that purpose is likely
to be counterproductive.

A young woman whose boyfriend had left her said she
could not understand why. "The relationship," she said,
"was more important than any substantive issue, so I gave

in immediately on everything." A psychiatrist tried to help her understand by saying something along the following lines: "It takes two to have a relationship. Where were you? If you gave in immediately on everything, what were you contributing? If your boyfriend wanted someone to engage him in a relationship, someone with interests and views to be taken into account, your giving in, no matter how simple or satisfying that may have seemed to him in the short run, must have made the overall relationship less satisfying."

Giving in does not build a good working relationship. It may avoid arguments, but it also eliminates the opportunity to learn how to talk through problems and to become skillful at reaching solutions. Without such skills, a relationship will be too weak to survive problems that are bound to come along. It is not enough to solve the immediate problem. We have to think ahead to the effect that this transaction will have on the next one, and the one after that. That is what building a relationship is all about.

Especially in business, some people try to buy relationships rather than build them. Granting a series of business "favors" can, it is true, sometimes make for easy access and preferential treatment, but it may also raise doubts. No one wants to rely on somebody who expects to buy his way out of future problems. And no one likes the feeling of being bribed.

In international matters, we are likely to recognize the danger of trying to build a relationship by appeasement. Chamberlain's mistaken belief that he had bought "peace in our time" by giving in to Hitler in 1938 at Munich is too deeply imbedded in our collective memory to leave that lesson unlearned.

The working relationship we seek, whether as individuals or nations, is a process for dealing with differences. It is a process involving reason, understanding, communication, reliability, noncoercive means of influence, and acceptance. Those qualities cannot be developed by giving in on substantive disputes. If we demonstrate that the other side can expect concessions from us, our process for solving disputes reasonably and equitably breaks down.

Trying to buy a relationship is like paying blackmail. The more blackmail I pay, the more I will be asked to pay. And neither paying blackmail nor extorting it is likely to prepare the way for fair outcomes in the future.

To be sure, I can enhance a working relationship by doing what I ought to do — by paying a debt to which you are legitimately entitled. But here the real issue is reliability. I am giving you something because you have a right to receive it. The relevant standard is what I owe, not what I hope will be enough to buy good behavior.

Two arguments are sometimes advanced to support the strategy of making substantive concessions as a way of building a working relationship. The first rests on the fact that the more substantive concessions either of us makes, the fewer issues will remain to be resolved. This is true, and it is often wise to concede something in order to settle one of a number of problems. Or, if you and I already have a good working relationship, we may both understand that if I make a concession today, you will return the favor in the future. But I should make a concession in order to get the benefits, all things considered, of settling that problem, not with the expectation that backing down will turn a poor working relationship into a good one.

The second argument for making a substantive concession is that since the other person wants a good relationship, he should pay something for it. But when two people can deal with their shared and conflicting interests efficiently and wisely, both benefit. There is no reason for either to make a unilateral substantive payment in order to establish a process that is *mutually* beneficial. Even if in the short term one will benefit from a good working relationship more than the other, both are sure to benefit in the long term. To ask a price for the relationship is likely to damage the very relationship being sought.

One explanation for our difficulty in building better relationships lies in our tendency to let our substantive interests themselves adversely affect the way we approach them. Either we let short-term concerns dominate our long-term concern for the way we interact, or we mix up our substantive differences with the process for dealing with them — by requesting a substantive concession as a way to improve that process or by granting one. The first step in building a working relationship is to disentangle those issues regarding the process for dealing with substantive problems from the problems themselves. We should then deal with each set of issues independently. On that premise, the next chapter develops a strategy or program for achieving the goal of a good working relationship.

3 | A Strategy

Be unconditionally constructive

CHAPTER I defined the sort of relationship that makes it easier to reconcile differences. Yet even when we understand the kind of relationship we need to get what we want, and even when we separate relationship from substantive issues, our actions may not lead us to a good working relationship.

Most of the time we carry on our various relationships without following any conscious strategy — specific rules of conduct or guidelines that we think will improve the relationship. We may simply react to what others do. Or emotions may dominate logic and keep us from pursuing any strategy we might have in mind. Sometimes, however, we will be following a deliberate strategy — a theory of how to have better relations — without realizing it is a poor one.

To achieve the kind of relationship we want, we are likely to need a few explicit guidelines. At a minimum, we will want to avoid two common mistakes.

1. Ignoring partisan perceptions. We forget how differently people can see things.

2. Relying on reciprocity. We try to build a relationship

by expecting others to follow our lead or by following theirs.

Beware of partisan perceptions; don't forget how differently people see things

Each of us needs the kind of relationship with someone else that will enable us to cope successfully with whatever problems come along. As I seek such a working relationship with you, there is a great risk that I will fail to appreciate how differently you view the world. If our disagreements are significant, we will almost certainly have strikingly dissimilar perceptions of ourselves, of each other, of what is important, of what our relationship is today, and of what it might become. Unless I understand these differences, they will interfere with our ability to solve problems.

Each of us tends to see things in ways that take our own interests disproportionately into account. And the facts we know best are those closest to us. The more we know about something, the more important it is likely to appear. An auto accident just outside our house is more important to us than an earthquake ten thousand miles away. A drizzle on our picnic looms larger in our lives than a typhoon in the Far East.

The process of perceiving things and building up our beliefs is highly personal. Each of us:

- observes different events;
- focuses attention on different aspects of these events;
- tends to concentrate on evidence that supports our prior views;
- filters and labels information so that it is easy to store;

- remembers information so that it fits a coherent "story"; and
- reshapes information previously stored to fit new needs.

Psychologists have found that all people, in varying degrees, need consistency in the way they relate their perceptions and their beliefs. There is a great deal of truth to the adage, "Where you stand depends on where you sit." Union leaders, looking at the facts of a labor-management dispute, may see underpaid workers, price inflation, and management hostility. Management may see highly paid workers, rising costs, and a history of union threats. Even two individuals whose lives are extremely close observe, note, and remember quite different things. For example, if we were to stop and read the minds of a middle manager and a higher executive on a Friday afternoon after a bad week, we might find them to have perceptions along the lines illustrated in the chart on the facing page.

Once their differences are brought to their attention, the middle manager and higher executive ought to be able to understand each other's perceptions without difficulty. When people in a relationship are further apart — in terms of distance, culture, background, and role — the contrast between their perceptions will be greater, and each will find it more difficult to appreciate how the other sees things.

A successful strategy for building a working relationship has to recognize that partisans will perceive their differences differently. In this respect, the U.S.-Soviet relationship is particularly difficult. Officials of the two countries,

Partisan Perceptions

A middle manager	A higher executive
The boss changes policy like a chameleon.	The people who work for me respond slowly to my directives.
There is far too much paper-work in this organization.	People are late with their monthly reports.
I work most evenings and weekends, yet my boss goes home at 6 P.M.	When I was at their level, I worked night and day to get a promotion.
This company rewards experience elsewhere. They bring in outsiders above me.	The people we train are deserting the company for competitors.
I can probably make more money somewhere else.	We are paying our people far more than I made at their age.
At a higher level, I would have some control over my life.	My subordinates have no idea of the pressure I am under.
We never hear about new policies until the last minute.	I never hear from my people about a problem until the last minute.
My boss doesn't trust me; he's always looking over my shoulder.	I'm breaking my back to spend time with my people and train them.
They don't appreciate what I do.	They don't appreciate what I do.

living in different cultures, observing some facts at close range and others at a distance, and approaching those facts with different ideologies, values, and interests, cannot possibly have the same perceptions.

Consider the element of reliability. Everyone recognizes that it is difficult to work with someone who cannot be trusted, someone who makes misleading statements or makes promises that are not fulfilled. The U.S.-Soviet problem, however, involves not just questionable reliability, but also highly different perceptions of reliability. To improve the working relationship between the two governments, we need a strategy that will work despite those conflicting perceptions. The objective truth about which is more reliable (as scientific investigators, historians, and legal scholars might later decide) is only one bit of data. In a given situation, it may not even be important. What is important is that we can predict with confidence that each government will see itself as being more reliable than the other, and certainly as being more reliable than the other perceives it to be.

The charts on pages 29 and 30 illustrate American and Soviet perceptions in 1987.

The fact that perceptions are going to differ, and with a strong partisan bias in favor of the side holding them, is a serious obstacle in building a relationship that can deal well with differences. Partisan perceptions about substantive matters create some differences and make others more difficult to solve.

Partisan perceptions about the way we interact can be even more damaging. If I value cooperation, understanding, and honesty, I am almost certain to see my conduct as more cooperative, more understanding, and more honest than you see it. Likewise, if I have serious differences with you,

Partisan perceptions

U.S. RELIABILITY

A U.S. view	A Soviet view
The Salt II treaty is not binding because it was never ratified.	The U.S. signed the Salt II treaty but then did not even ask for Senate approval.
The U.S. is free to reinterpret the language of the ABM Treaty since the Soviets would be free to do so.	The U.S. signed the ABM Treaty and then, 14 years later, "reinterpreted" it in a way contrary to what all the negotiators and the U.S. Senate understood.
Since no comprehensive test ban treaty has been concluded, the U.S. is free to continue testing.	The U.S. signed the Non-Proliferation Treaty, committing it to seek an end to all nuclear testing for all time. It now ignores that obligation, saying that it wants to continue testing as long as nuclear weapons exist.
In view of Soviet threats and subversion, the U.S. must be free to act in self-defense against terrorism and aggression.	The U.S. treats itself as free to violate international law by mining Nicaraguan harbors, bombing Libya, and using force to try to overthrow even legal governments that it recognizes.

Partisan perceptions

SOVIET RELIABILITY

A U.S. view	A Soviet view
The radar facility at Krasnoyarsk constitutes a violation of the Anti-Ballistic Missile Treaty.	The radar facility is a space-tracking device permitted by the ABM Treaty.
A number of Soviet nuclear tests constitute likely violations of the 150-kiloton limit set by the 1974 Threshold Test Ban Treaty.	U.S. studies consistently overestimate the magnitude of Soviet nuclear tests. Unofficial American experts agree that none has exceeded the 150-kiloton limit.
The Soviet Union consistently violates its promises.	The Soviet Union carefully honors its legal obligations.
They care nothing for the spirit of an agreement.	We adhere to the letter of every treaty.

I am likely to see your behavior as lacking those qualities. As a result, I am likely to blame you for problems in the relationship and to justify my own faults as better than yours: "You never listen to me, so it's not worth talking to you." When partisan perceptions create negative reactions in the relationship, it deteriorates.

As the next section points out, the consequences of partisan perceptions are particularly acute if either side uses reciprocity as a guide for behavior.

Don't rely on reciprocity to build a relationship by expecting others to follow our lead or by following theirs

The good relationship that we seek is reciprocal. Two people will deal more skillfully with their differences if both behave rationally, both fully understand each other's perceptions, both communicate effectively, both are reliable, neither tries to coerce the other, and each accepts the other as someone whose interests and views deserve to be taken into account.

The principle of reciprocity is familiar in substantive negotiations, where a favor or concession by one side is exchanged for a similar favor or concession by the other. If I shovel the snow off my neighbor's walk when he is away in the winter, I can fairly ask him to mow my lawn when I am away in the summer. Fairness suggests that if the Soviet Union asks the United States to cut its nuclear missiles by 50 percent, it should offer to cut its own missiles by the same percentage. We may disagree about exactly what is reciprocal. (If you did me a favor by driving my children home from school last week, do I owe you the favor of looking after your son, Buster, all day Saturday?) But the principle of reciprocity is a generally accepted external standard of fairness in substantive negotiations.

Since a reciprocal relationship is our goal, and since reciprocity is a sound basis for substantive agreements, there is a natural tendency to rely on some form of reciprocity as the key to building an effective working relationship. This tendency, however, is dangerous. In one form, a reciprocal strategy looks like an application of the Golden Rule: "Do unto others as you would have them do unto you." In another form, it constitutes a hostile policy of "an eye for an eye": I will treat you as badly as you have been treating me. Either policy is risky.

The Golden Rule. The Golden Rule is a useful rule of

thumb in helping me understand how my behavior is likely to affect you and how you might want me to behave. If you, as a middle manager, appreciate being consulted by your superiors before they make major decisions that affect you, then you can safely predict that I, a subordinate, would like similar treatment. But the Golden Rule is *not* based on the premise that if I behave as you would like, I can safely predict that you will behave the same way. If I avoid criticizing you in public, I cannot safely assume that you will avoid criticizing me. If I try to build a working relationship based on such an optimistic view — that you will reciprocate my

---

An Extreme Application of the Golden Rule

---

1. **Rationality.** Since I would like you to base your actions on love for me, I will base all my actions, not on reason, but on love for you.

2. **Understanding.** Since I would like you to accept my understanding of the situation as correct, I will accept yours.

3. **Communication.** Since I would like you not to bother me with problems, there is no need to talk about any of our differences.

4. **Reliability.** Since I would like you to trust me completely, I will trust you completely.

5. **Coercion/Persuasion.** Since I would like you to yield to me, I will yield to you.

6. **Acceptance.** Since I would like you to accept my interests and views as controlling, I will accept yours as controlling.

---

actions — I will make dangerous mistakes. This can be seen by examining how such a strategy would apply to each of the qualities identified in the last chapter as being important to a good working relationship.

No one seriously recommends this strategy — although some who work for better relations are accused of doing so, and others may favor bits of it, such as not talking about differences. To pursue a comprehensive approach resting on the premise that others will follow our example is highly risky and unwise. I might think I want your actions to be based wholly on affection for me, but we will not solve serious differences if I act wholly on the basis of affection for you. I may *think* that I would like you to accept without question my understanding of a situation, but it will not help us deal with reality for me to accept yours. As unpleasant as discussing differences may sometimes be, it is the only way to deal with them successfully. And if we were to trust everybody simply because we would like everybody to trust us, we would certainly be disappointed — and broke. Reliance on reciprocal good will is not a sound foundation on which to build a working relationship.

This is particularly true when partisan perceptions are taken into account. If I pursue a strategy that depends on your equivalent behavior, I will probably find that you fail the test. Even if you believe your behavior is as good as mine, I am likely to see it as worse. I may then become discouraged and turn to a different, more hostile strategy.

An eye for an eye. To avoid the obvious risks of expecting reciprocity, some people propose using reciprocity as leverage. They suggest that I let you take the lead. If and when you treat me well, I will treat you the same way. In the meantime, I will do to you whatever you are doing to me. This policy, too, is based on an application of the principle

of reciprocity. In a personal context, it might be summarized as follows:

An Eye for an Eye

---

1. **Reason and emotion.** Since anger dominates your thinking,
   it will dominate mine.

2. **Understanding.** Since you misunderstand me, I will put the
   worst interpretation on what you do — a prescription certain to produce misunderstanding.

3. **Communication.** Since you are not listening to me, I will
   not listen to you.

4. **Reliability.** Since you are apparently trying to deceive me,
   I will try to deceive you.

5. **Noncoercive modes of influence.** Since you are trying to
   coerce me, I will try to coerce you.

6. **Acceptance.** Since you are denigrating me, my views, and
   my interests, I will denigrate you and yours.

Such an approach may be the result of my asking why I
should behave better than you do. Or perhaps it rests on
the notion that only by punishing your bad behavior can I
get you to behave better. Regardless, such a strategy is no
way to turn a poor working relationship into a good one. If
I let my conduct in the relationship reflect yours, we may
never break out of a pattern of hostile interaction. If I react
to your bad behavior with actions that are equally bad, I
end up accepting the destructive tone you have set.

Again, the effect of partisan perceptions makes matters
worse. I am almost certain to see your conduct as worse

than mine. If my strategy is to duplicate your conduct and your strategy is to duplicate mine, the bias of partisan perceptions will cause our relationship to deteriorate in a downward spiral. I, putting a bad interpretation on your conduct, duplicate it. Then you, putting an equally partisan interpretation on my conduct, follow my lead and worsen your conduct. Communication breaks down, misunderstanding increases, and trust disappears.

A clear example in personal relations is seen when two people each wait for an apology from the other. As time passes, each becomes more upset with the other and more certain about not apologizing first. Any belated, and possibly grudging, apology may be unable to put to rest a problem that could have been cleared up quickly.

In easily quantifiable situations, such as the expulsion of one low-ranking diplomat suspected of spying, an "eye for an eye" policy may not get out out of hand. In more important and more ambiguous situations — when, for example, in arms control or divorce negotiations each party is uncertain whether the other is pursuing negotiations in good faith, honestly disclosing relevant information, or advancing proposals seriously — a partisan interpretation of the other's conduct combined with a policy of following suit will cause an ever-decreasing ability to solve problems.

In any event, by behaving as badly as you do, I abandon a leadership role. I give up the enormous opportunity I have to set the tone and manner of our interaction. If each side in a relationship waits for the other to improve first, there will be no improvement. Reactive reciprocity makes it extremely difficult to deal well with differences. (For those interested in Game Theory, a note at the back of this book reconciles what is said here with arguments that have been advanced in favor of a simplified policy, dubbed "tit-for-tat.")

We have considered two basic explanations for why we often fail to build a good working relationship: we suffer from partisan bias; and we operate on a reciprocal basis. Either factor alone can frustrate a strategy for building a better relationship. Together, they are almost certain to do so.

Requirements of a successful strategy

If the analysis in these first three chapters is sound, a strategy for building a better working relationship must pass some difficult tests:

Independent of disagreement. In no way should our guidelines require substantive agreement. While agreement makes relationships more comfortable, the more serious our disagreements, the more we need a good working relationship to cope with them. We need an "all weather" strategy.

Independent of concessions. Our strategy should neither require us to give in nor demand that others do so.

Independent of partisan perceptions. We should take into account the extent to which we and they will see things differently. The value of our guidelines should not rest on the premise that we see the truth and they are wrong. Although on each occasion we may firmly believe that we are right, it is impossible to build a relationship on the premise that the other side is always wrong.

Independent of reciprocity. We should not wait for the other side to engage in exemplary behavior, nor should we assume that our example will be followed.

Independent of permanent "sides." If our goal involves full understanding and being open to persuasion, a good strategy should also leave us open to revising our views about who is on our side and who is not. Just as a neighbor may become a member of the family, so business adversaries may become joint venturers and former enemies may become military allies. Relationship-building should be open-ended.

A prescriptive approach: be unconditionally constructive

The balance of this chapter outlines a strategy that meets the tests set out above. This is no miracle strategy that will turn criminals into trustworthy friends, business adversaries into reliable colleagues, and enemies into allies. No such strategy exists. What we offer is a framework for thinking about the problem, a general approach that seems to make sense, and some rules of thumb that may prove helpful in many situations.

In any relationship, I want to be able to take steps that will both improve our ability to work together and advance my substantive interests, whether or not you respond as I would like. In short, I am looking for guidelines I can follow that will be both good for the relationship and good for me, *whether or not you follow the same guidelines*. In that sense, this strategy is "unconditionally constructive."

Finally, because we will be better able to settle our differences wisely and easily if both of us approach the relationship constructively, I would like the guidelines to be good for you, too. In fact, I would like them to be the best that you could follow. They should be as good for you as they are for me.

To meet these rigorous tests, the strategy cannot be as bold, trusting, and venturesome as some would like. It must be risk averse. (We, the authors, do not know with whom you, the readers, may be dealing.) In some circumstances, it will not be as quick or successful in improving a relationship as a bolder — and riskier — approach might be. In baldest outline, it is as follows:

An Unconditionally Constructive Strategy

Do only those things that are both good for the relationship
and good for us,
whether or not they reciprocate.

1. **Rationality.** Even if they are acting emotionally,
   balance emotions with reason.

2. **Understanding.** Even if they misunderstand us,
   try to understand them.

3. **Communication.** Even if they are not listening,
   consult them before deciding on matters that affect them.

4. **Reliability.** Even if they are trying to deceive us, neither
   trust them nor deceive them;
   be reliable.

5. **Noncoercive modes of influence.** Even if they are trying to
   coerce us, neither yield to that coercion nor try to
   coerce them;
   be open to persuasion and try to persuade them.

6. **Acceptance.** Even if they reject us and our concerns as unworthy of their consideration,
   accept them as worthy of our consideration,
   care about them, and
   be open to learning from them.

These guidelines are not advice on how to be "good," but
rather on how to be effective. They derive from a selfish,
hard-headed concern with what each of us can do, in practical terms, to make a relationship work better. The high
moral content of the guidelines is a bonus. I can feel good
about improving the way we deal with differences.

In every relationship, we are bound to encounter significant conflicts of interest. But we will almost always share an interest in dealing skillfully with those conflicts. Neither partner in a relationship wants the other to bungle. It is not inconsistent for me to want to advance selfish interests that conflict with yours and at the same time want to improve our joint ability to deal with those conflicting interests.

In terms of a two-person relationship, the chart on the following page suggests why each element of this suggested approach might be good for both the relationship and my substantive interests.

You and I can each pursue this strategy without risk to our substantive interests. No matter how you respond to my behavior, I will tend to be better off than if I were to pursue another strategy. And if you follow the strategy, no matter how I respond to your behavior, you will tend to be better off.

Each of the next six chapters is devoted to one of the six basic elements of the relationship goal. Each element is both a critical aspect of a working relationship and a critical aspect of the strategy for building that kind of relationship.

Unconditionally Constructive

Unconditionally constructive advice:	Good for the relationship because:	Good for me because:
1. Balance emotion with reason.	An irrational battle is less likely.	I make fewer mistakes.
2. Try to understand.	The better I understand you, the fewer collisions we will have.	The less I shoot in the dark, the better solutions I can invent and the better able I am to influence you.
3. Inquire, consult, and listen.	We both participate in making decisions. Better communication improves them.	I reduce the risk of making a mistake without giving up the ability to decide.
4. Be reliable.	It tends to build trust and confidence.	My words will have more impact.
5. Be open to persuasion; try to persuade.	If people are persuaded rather than coerced, both the outcome and compliance are better.	By being open, I keep learning; it is easier to resist coercion if one is open to persuasion.
6. Accept the other as worth dealing with and learning from.	To deal well with our differences, I have to deal with you and have an open mind.	By dealing with you and reality, I remove obstacles to learning the facts and to persuading you on the merits.

II Basic Elements of a Working Relationship

4 | Rationality

Balance emotions with reason

TO VARYING DEGREES, emotions affect all our relationships. They affect how we think and how we behave. Whether in a chance encounter or on meeting an old friend, we are likely to feel a response to the way the other person looks, smiles, sounds, or shakes hands. Emotions run the gamut from those we tend to think of as positive, such as love, admiration, respect, and concern, to those we tend to think of as negative, such as fear, hate, anger, and guilt. But whether we like them or not, emotions happen. We do not choose our feelings, and we should no more make a moral judgment about feeling angry than we should about feeling cold or hungry. What we can affect and what we should judge is behavior — how we express our emotions.

Emotions can help a relationship. They give us information about ourselves and others. Affection and empathy can motivate us to settle differences, but so can frustration or anxiety. Concern and sympathy may improve our listening. Anger may lead us to work hard in a constructive way.

On the other hand, strong emotions of any kind may lead us to behave in ways that impede our ability to deal with differences. Fear or grief may overcome logical thinking. Anger may make me unwilling to work with you on a joint problem. Even love can damage a working relationship if it leads me to give in too readily to your wishes in ways that we later regret.

Rational decision-making requires a balance

Every problem, large or small, has an emotional aspect. Two people should be able to think clearly about their differences while they feel and cope with emotions of different kinds and intensities. Their emotions should not cause them to lose the ability to consider the pros and cons of a range of options before making a decision — whether the issue is sharing the family car, settling a lawsuit, working out a divorce, reworking a contract in light of changed market conditions, or negotiating a cease-fire between countries. In every case, emotions and reason should each be informed, but not overwhelmed, by the other.

Too much emotion can cloud judgment. We rarely think clearly when our emotions are running high. If a father is angry over his son's late return of the car — with the gas tank almost empty — he is probably not in the best frame of mind to work out fair rules for the future use of the car. If an employee fears being fired at the same time her boss is upset after an argument with his wife, the two are unlikely to deal well with any significant differences.

Some people are easily overwhelmed by emotion. For them, anxiety over an upcoming test, going to the dentist, or taking a trip may be enough to interfere with sound decision-making. Others can concentrate and reason clearly despite serious worries or recent quarrels. But all of us, at one time or another, will be so upset that we will find it difficult, if not impossible, to deal wisely with a conflict.

The more intense our emotions, the more likely they are

to overwhelm our reason. The more deeply you love or respect someone, the angrier you will be if you believe that person to be criticized unfairly, and the less able you will be to refute the critic effectively. A small business owner facing bankruptcy if his employees strike may be less able to deal reasonably with a union in the face of hostile threats than would the president of a large conglomerate, for whom a strike would not be devastating. And the depth of terror felt by some white South Africans at the prospect of "majority rule" — which they equate with chaos and economic collapse — intensifies the difficulty they have in dealing wisely with the current situation. Ironically, their fears make it difficult for them to consider the small practical steps that might help remove the basis for those fears.

Even emotions we consider positive can interfere with good problem-solving. Excessive feelings of loyalty and enthusiasm for President Reagan's agenda led Lieutenant Colonel Oliver North to break the law and deceive Congress. The testimony of White House officials suggests that President Reagan's sympathy for the hostages in Lebanon influenced his decision to ship arms to Iran in violation of common sense, an established embargo, and his own declared policy.

Seiji Ozawa, the conductor of the Boston Symphony Orchestra, once explained why his collaboration with the orchestra had not always reached its full potential: "Because of my very long relationship with the orchestra, and my deep respect for the players, I found it difficult to ask for everything I wanted" (*Boston Globe,* December 6, 1987, p. A25). In business, enthusiasm for a potential deal may lead negotiators to pay little attention to important details. All of us have offered something in the glow of friendship or enthusiasm that we have later, on reflection, regretted.

Strong emotions may blur not only our own thinking, but

the thinking of those with whom we are dealing. The teen-age daughter whose mother screams at her in anger is likely to feel anger in return. She may shout back or run away, but in either case she and her mother will be less able to deal with their immediate difference. Most of us, when faced with an emotional accusation, are probably more likely to react with anger and rejection than with calm understanding and reasoned discourse.

When emotions in a relationship dominate thought, we are likely to see a downward spiral of destructive behavior. The more important the conflicting interests at stake, the more intense the emotional reactions are likely to be. Management may fire striking workers; workers may sabotage company equipment. For years, the arms race between the United States and Soviet Union has accelerated while fear and mistrust dominated the thinking of each government.

Too little emotion impairs motivation and understanding. While strong emotions may exacerbate a problem, the answer is not simply to suppress them. Emotions are the root of motivation. We would all rather do something because we enjoy it or feel challenged than because we "have to." Most successful companies seek to involve their employees emotionally as well as economically. They have found that an honest concern for employees and their problems creates high morale and an emotional commitment that improves productivity and teamwork. When poorly managed companies fail to enlist the support of employees to overcome a problem, they often hear the response, "Why should we go out of our way to help the company? What's in it for us?"

Emotions and emotional sensitivity are also important to our effectiveness in problem-solving. We would like our actions to be well reasoned and make sense, but each element of a good working relationship depends on emotional input. Our understanding of another person's perceptions and interests will be inadequate unless it is empathetic — unless we know, to some degree at least, what it *feels* like to be in that situation. If we don't understand how others are feeling, our communication may suffer. Only if we recognize how they feel about things will we be able to persuade them. Finally, a full acceptance of another person as someone whose interests and views matter depends on our feelings of caring and respect.

Without appropriate emotions — including some caring by each side for the welfare of the other — it may be impossible for people to resolve important conflicts. If your spouse is feeling ignored and unappreciated, an affable, "Do whatever you want, dear," may only make things worse. An exclusive reliance on cold rationality as a means of understanding the world denies us access to important realms of human experience, without which we may be unable to deal with a difference effectively. Emotions give us clues about how we are being treated and what we need. An ignored and unappreciated husband may be less in need of an explanation of why he feels that way than of a weekend with his wife away from work and children. In any family, hugs may be more useful than lectures.

The emotional involvement in a working relationship is thus two-sided: the ability to deal with differences will be damaged to the extent that strong emotions overwhelm reason. That ability will be enhanced if reason is informed, enlightened, and supported by a positive emotional commitment to joint problem-solving. But achieving that working balance in practice may not be easy. Why? And, given the obstacles, what is the best way for us to achieve an adequate balance of emotion and reason?

How can we balance emotions and reason?

The interactions among emotions and reason are infinitely complex, and we, the authors, are not psychologists, but experience and common sense suggest some basic problems and what we can do about them.

The reasons we have difficulty in balancing emotion and reason can usefully be sorted into four categories. First, we may be unaware of our own emotional state and that of others. Second, even if we are usually aware of our emotions, there are times when they will surge within us so quickly or so strongly that they will take charge of our behavior. Third, even when our reasoning self is aware of our emotions and in charge of our behavior, we may not deal well with those emotions. We may try to hide them or deny their existence, and they may resurface to bother us later. Finally, an underlying reason for all these difficulties is that we do not prepare for our emotions before they arise.

The rest of this chapter examines each of these difficulties in turn and suggests some unconditionally constructive things that we can do about them.

Develop an awareness of emotions — ours and theirs. We are often unaware of feelings. Insecurity, frustration, fear, or anger can take hold and begin to affect our actions without our realizing what is happening. Someone else may notice that my neck muscles have tightened, my face has begun to flush, or an edge has crept into my voice long before I recognize anger in myself.

I may be even less aware of your emotions. If you are angry or afraid, you may not show it openly, but it is likely to affect your behavior in subtle ways: the tone of your voice, the way you sit, the rhythm of your breathing. Subconsciously, I may note these signals and respond to them, so that I too feel uncomfortable, afraid, or obstinate. If neither of us recognizes our own feelings or the other's, it will be difficult indeed to control how we express them. And if we cannot control how we express our emotions, we are unlikely to deal well with the substantive issues that brought us together.

A first step, then, in dealing constructively with emotions is to become aware of them. One way is to practice reading the emotional signals in our bodies. By paying attention to different parts of my body, I can get important clues about my feelings. Does my stomach feel tight or upset? Are my palms moist? Are my jaw muscles clenched? Am I making fists or gripping something tightly? Am I raising my voice? These are all possible signals of anger, frustration, or fear. A soft voice, a tendency to move closer, and moist eyes can indicate affection, empathy, or perhaps sadness. Depending on the context, my physical sensations may indicate different emotions. But once I have noted the sensations, identifying the underlying emotion is usually not difficult.

To develop a habit of awareness, I may want to practice in a variety of contexts and under increasing degrees of stress. I might start with just one or two careful inventories each day — during dinner with friends, while negotiating with a client, when watching a sad movie, or just after a difficult discussion — to develop a sense of my emotional and sensory repertoire. As I come to understand how my body reacts, such checks become easier and quicker, and I may make them more frequently or try them out in more stressful situations.

It may be more difficult for me to become aware of your emotions because my information is more limited. I can see what you are doing with your body and listen to your voice, but I don't know what you are thinking and may guess wrongly about what you are feeling. Still, your physical cues can sometimes tell me whether something important is going on emotionally. If I were in your situation, handling my body as you are and speaking with your tone of voice, how would I be feeling? The more I know about how you feel, the more I will be able to avoid insensitive remarks or acts that may reinforce hostile feelings or squander constructive ones. As a general rule, it makes sense to survey the emotional terrain with someone before dealing with the substance of a problem.

While practice and training in observation can increase my sensitivity to physical and vocal cues, there will always be some ambiguity. To find out for sure what you are feeling, I may want to check my conclusions with you: "John, it looks as if you are about to dig holes into the arm of that chair, and I feel as though I was snapped at after my last question. Have I done something to make you angry?" Body language is ambiguous, and we are each prone to see things from a partisan point of view. It is better for me to make a good guess about your feelings than to ignore them, but it is risky to act on the basis of an untested assumption. The chance of miscommunication is high. If I check out my guess without being accusatory or judgmental, I may avoid misunderstanding and make it easier for you to say what is really on your mind.

Becoming aware of feelings helps me step above the emotional fray. With practice I can, for a moment, adopt the stance of a detached observer with enough perspective to analyze the emotions present and think of ways of dealing with them. This process of distancing can also reduce the effect on my behavior that my feelings might otherwise have. Distancing can make it easier for reason to play a balancing role.

Don't react emotionally; take charge of our behavior. An awareness of my emotions may not be enough to control my behavior; my emotions may lead me to react before I have consciously decided what to do. Psychologists believe that in the course of evolution, the early brain produced our instinctive and emotional reactions. The more rational brain developed later and attained the power to override many low-level instinctive reactions. But threatening circumstances may trigger emotional and physiological reactions that "short-circuit" our rational process. Even mild levels of fear or mistrust may cause us to behave in ways — like running away — that protect us in the short run but are counterproductive to thoughtful problem-solving. Fear of abandonment may lead to similar responses. If a wife threatens to leave her husband, he may react with anger or rejection. Neither emotional response is likely to help solve the issues that led to his wife's threat.

Threats to self-esteem often create feelings of insecurity, fear, and rage, which become a barrier to rational problem-solving. People who have low self-esteem, or who fear a loss of self-esteem, are usually more reluctant than most to change their minds in a dispute. They fear losing face and may act in ways that postpone accommodation and worsen the eventual outcome. Examples of this situation include the refusal of white South Africans to negotiate with blacks and the difficulty a doubting fiancé may have in breaking his engagement.

In the Middle East, Israeli and Arab reactions to the trauma that each has suffered produce feelings that have prevented even the beginning of a working relationship. Even if two governments reach an agreement, fear may lead one side or both to ignore it. Fear of Libya may help explain why the leaders of Morocco and Egypt have failed to unify their countries with Libya, even though they signed agreements to do so.

Some of our emotional reactions are not instinctive, but habits that we have learned from parents or friends. As children, many of us learned that emotional outbursts bring attention and change and that losing our temper is at times an acceptable and excusable way of expressing frustration, anger, or disappointment. We may carry into adulthood the implicit belief that we get what we want if we have temper tantrums, behave outrageously, shout, slam doors, or issue orders.

An emotional concern with losing may outweigh the potential benefits of an agreement. Some of us deal with the fear of failure by giving up and not trying to win. Others learn as children that it is easier to disrupt a game by kicking over the table than to lose. Most of us learn that if we disrupt the game every time we are losing, no one will want to play with us. But many adults continue to disrupt negotiations that do not turn in their favor.

At times we may unconsciously let our emotions take over to avoid blame for failures or mistakes. Many of us have seen a car accident in which the driver at fault starts shouting at the other, innocent, driver. As the shouting driver becomes more and more emotionally committed to his innocence, he may succeed in convincing both himself and any bystanders that he *is* free of blame. He is using his emotions, perhaps unconsciously, to escape blame and guilt.

In other cases, we may consciously try to use our emotions to coerce others. If a hotel clerk tells me that he has lost my reservation and that there are no rooms available, I may blow up, slam my fist on the counter, and ask for the manager. I may be assuming that this will get me a room — and maybe it will, since the cost to the hotel of having a hysterical person in the lobby is high. But if I behave this way with someone with whom I wish to maintain a relationship, I am likely to be counterproductive. In the long run, emotional coercion will cause more problems than it solves.

Use some common techniques to buy time. We cannot expect to get rid of strong emotions surging within us, nor should we want to, but we *can* control their influence on our behavior. If the decisions we make in a relationship are to have the full benefit of our rational thinking, we will want to postpone them until our judgment is not overwhelmed by strong emotions — until we are in charge of our behavior. Some specific techniques for doing so include:

Take a break. The easiest technique for minimizing the impact of strong emotions is to interrupt the encounter for a short break. When tempers flare or frustration builds, a well-placed break can prevent the complete deterioration of the relationship. It offers both sides an opportunity to cool down, recall the possible benefits of an ongoing relationship, and think through ways to handle the current issue that won't trigger disruptive anger in the other person. A break may allow us to work together on more immediate problems — fixing the coffee machine, getting some fresh air into the room — and change how we interact with each other.

During a heated discussion, I may find it difficult to pull away for a moment of reflection. If this is likely, I may ask a third person to monitor the emotions of the discussion and suggest breaks when they seem appropriate. In some families, one parent plays this role.

Count to ten. We want to think before acting. Since emotions can take over quickly, before we are aware of them, we often act under their control without thinking. Our hasty actions are likely to cause disruptive emotional states in the other person; the interaction may deteriorate to a level at which productive work is impossible. In some situations, it will be enough to count to ten, force ourselves to think about what might have prompted the other person's statement, and plan a response that will shift the discussion to a more productive level. Before responding, it is always useful to ask oneself: "At this point, what is my purpose?"

Consult. The danger of my behaving in ways that reflect strong emotion rather than rational concern is increased when I act alone. As discussed in Chapter 6, on communication, it is generally a good idea for me to consult my partner in a relationship before acting in ways that significantly affect both of us. If emotions are running too high or if other circumstances preclude such consultation, I might ask a friend or colleague for advice. Is my proposed action sensible? What are the risks? Might something else be better?

With each of these techniques, the point is not to suppress or ignore my emotions. I should no more ignore them than I should ignore any other important fact in a negotiation. But my emotional state may cause me to make poor judgments about what to say and what to do. A break or consultation will allow me to acknowledge my emotions to myself, learn from them, and take charge of my behavior.

Acknowledge emotions. Even if I am aware of my emotions and can take charge of my behavior sufficiently to avoid an immediate harmful reaction, the emotions themselves remain and may cause problems in the future. Some of us try to hide our emotions, even from ourselves. If others notice that my voice is getting louder, I may try to bury my feelings and deny them. I may shout, "I am *NOT* angry!" convincing everyone more than ever that I am. But denying emotions doesn't make them go away. It just makes them harder to deal with. We may try to hide emotions for many reasons. We may have learned as children not to show or talk about feelings. Some families treat all emotions as problems. Some children are taught that it is naughty to show anger and wrong to show sadness. All too often, the children learn that feeling angry or sad is wrong, too, and they grow up learning to suppress their feelings.

Sometimes whole cultures develop an ethic of suppressing emotions and emotional display. The English are often portrayed as paragons of cool and unflappable reserve. Their language is peppered with phrases that reflect the control of emotional expression: "stiff upper lip," "steady on," "bite the bullet." Business environments vary dramatically — from banks and law firms, where juniors are likely to learn to cover up their feelings, to docksides and the commodities trading floors, where emotions may be expressed even more strongly than they are felt.

Many of us hide our emotions because we fear the consequences of showing them. If we show anger or disappointment, we may not be liked. If we show empathy, it may be seen as a sign of weakness. The press gave repeated coverage to photographs of the political candidates Edmund Muskie and Patricia Schroeder, each wiping away a tear, as though that might reveal some serious character defect. Fear that an accurate display of feeling will be seen as a weakness can dramatically affect international relations, where there is often a special concern with appearing strong. Although showing an excess of emotion may sometimes be a sign that I have lost control of myself, most of us are more likely to err on the side of showing too little emotion than too much.

The tendency to hide our emotions causes two problems in a relationship. First, unless we can reveal our feelings, at least to ourselves, we cannot deal with them. Potentially destructive feelings like anger and resentment can fester until they flare into an outburst that causes long-term damage to a relationship. Furthermore, when we hide our feelings, we may be ignoring underlying substantive problems that need attention.

Second, we conceal the supportive emotions necessary for a working relationship. Many corporate managers fail, for example, because they do not show emotional concern for their employees. A manager who appears detached and aloof, even if he feels concern inside, is unlikely to engender the enthusiasm, loyalty, and openness necessary for a dynamic and effective organization.

Talk about emotions. One way to deal with emotions that may be disrupting a relationship is to make them explicit — to acknowledge and talk about them. Talking about one's anger or fear (in contrast to displaying it) tends to demonstrate self-confidence and self-control, not weakness. Talking about our emotions if we are not used to it can be uncomfortable. It may help to keep the following points in mind:

- Be explicit. "Excuse me, but this is beginning to make me angry."
- Talk with feeling. Establish eye contact, lower your voice, speak slowly, and let pauses emphasize your meaning. "I am so upset . . . that I am finding it difficult to focus on the terms of this deal. . . . I think we should find a way to change the tone of these discussions."
- Be specific. Illustrate what may be causing the feeling. "I am becoming frustrated. When I tried to explain my interest in a security deposit, I was interrupted in midsentence. When I tried to be constructive and suggest a mediator, the response, if I recall correctly, was, 'Can't you handle this yourself?'"
- Avoid blame. "I may have misinterpreted what you were saying. If I have done anything to upset you, I apologize."
- Check it out. "Please tell me if you heard our conversation differently."
- Provide an easy way out. "I know you have as much interest in settling this matter as I do. Perhaps, after you

have had a chance to respond a bit, we can take a break
and come back in ten minutes to the pros and cons of a
security deposit."

The advice is *not* simply to express feelings but to acknowledge their existence and to explain them to my partner in the relationship. That way, feelings will not stand in
the way of a good working relationship that can deal with
any difference on the merits. I'm not interested in scoring
points or just letting off steam. (I can let off steam in the
hallway or with a colleague.) I would like to clear the air
and get us both back to work. That means I should make it
as easy as possible for you to say or do something
constructive.

Talking rationally about my emotions almost automatically puts reason in charge. I am more likely to filter my
own reactions through a rational thought process. I may
also stimulate similar self-control in you.

Accept responsibility and apologize. We often fail to take
responsibility for our feelings because we blame them on
the other person in a relationship: "If I'm getting emotional, it's because you are being unreasonable."

To some extent, of course, this may be true. But we are
likely to see the other person as emotional and irrational,
even though we probably seem equally irrational to them.
It is normal for us to feel that we are being more rational
and even-tempered. We understand and sympathize with
our own beliefs and actions and — if we recognize them —
our emotions. Our feelings and actions make sense to us.
When we do not understand the concerns of others, we are
likely to see their actions and emotions as irrational. How
can we deal with irrational people?

We also fail to acknowledge the extent to which we may
be responsible for the other person's feelings. We may at-

tribute emotionality to character: "Oh, don't worry about him, he's just a hothead." We may think that there is nothing *we* can do to improve the relationship until *he* calms down.

If we fail to understand how we might be contributing to another person's emotional overload, we may behave in ways that make it worse. Consider the case of a tenant who went to see her landlord about the leaking roof after three letters had gone unanswered. The tenant was angry and began to yell at the landlord. The landlord turned his back and said that he wouldn't listen until the tenant stopped yelling. This made the tenant even angrier, since it was the landlord's failure to listen and respond that had made her angry in the first place. If the landlord had said, "I can see that you're angry. I'm sorry I did not get back to you sooner. Sit down and tell me exactly what the problem is," the tenant might well have become more reasonable.

It is usually a good idea to take responsibility for our own emotions, for how we express them, and for our impact on the feelings of others. If we do, we will be better able to defuse emotional outbursts and deal with problems rationally. If we have lost control of our emotions or triggered a strong emotional response in our relationship partner, an apology may help. An apology acknowledges responsibility, whether partial or full, demonstrates concern, and may bring a corresponding acceptance of responsibility from the other side which will allow a relationship to return to working order.

Too often, we equate an apology with a plea of guilty. And if we don't feel guilty, we don't want to apologize. It is possible, however, to express regret for the consequences caused by some action or omission on our part — whether or not the behavior or its consequences were intended. Rather than defend our behavior, we can ask that it be forgiven. Instead of saying, "I was busy," we can say, "I'm afraid that my mind was on something else. I'm sorry." Instead of saying, "It's not my fault," we can say, "I can see why you are upset, and to the extent that that's the result of my actions, I am sorry."

We all have strong feelings. We need not be afraid to show them, accept responsibility for them, and deal with them. Unless we do so, we are likely to leave burning an underground fire that may erupt at any time and damage our ability to work with others.

Prepare for emotions before they arise. Emotional reactions disrupt our reason in part because we have not anticipated and planned for them. They catch us by surprise. Lawyers who recognize this problem often spend time before a divorce proceeding counseling a client about what to expect and trying to anticipate how he or she might feel. If the lawyer can foresee that a client might be made angry or distraught by a particular question, the lawyer might suggest ways to respond or might counsel the client not to answer at all. Preparation not only provides a client with a way to deal with a strong emotion, it tends to reduce the emotion itself. Being prepared, the client is not surprised and is less upset.

Hard as it is to anticipate our own emotional reactions, it may be harder still to anticipate the reactions of the other person in a relationship. We may hear friends say, "I don't know what happened. I told him how I felt and he blew his lid." Since it is impossible for us to put ourselves into the emotional "skin" of another person, we may not try at all. But if we don't think about the other person's emotional state, we will blunder into emotional traps that we might have avoided had we taken the time to consider how we might feel in the other's position.

Perhaps most important, we do not think prospectively

about what emotional state we would like to be in, and what emotional state we would like our relationship partner to be in, to facilitate problem-solving. If we know that emotions play a large role in the outcome of a negotiation or dispute, it only makes sense to think as much about ways to influence the emotional state in a negotiation as about other strategies. This is especially true since the feelings we have toward the other person are likely to influence not only the current problem, but future problems as well.

Anticipate emotional reactions. By anticipating possible feelings we can improve the way we deal with them once they occur. This means that we need to think broadly about different problems that might come up. Good preparation for a negotiation does not consist of laying out a single path through the woods but of learning the terrain. When a thoughtful negotiator prepares for a meeting with a neighbor, a business contact, or a representative of another government, he will try to anticipate the proposals each will make and logical responses to them. But even the best negotiators all too often fail to anticipate their own emotional reactions, or those of their counterparts, to what may happen at the meeting.

One way to improve my preparation for a negotiation would be to sketch an emotional profile of myself and my counterpart. What makes me angry? How do I react to anger? How do I feel and behave when I am frustrated? What are the warning signs when I begin to abandon rational thinking? How does my counterpart behave under pressure? What makes her angry? How quickly does she tend to recover from emotional outbursts? Is there anything in my approach to this problem that may upset her? What might she say that would upset me?

Just as we prepare to handle substantive issues, we should prepare to handle emotional issues. If we spend some time before an encounter thinking about how we might react and how the other person might react, we will be better able to calm an emotional disruption when it occurs.

Recruit constructive emotions. Just as we often fail to anticipate troublesome emotional reactions in a negotiation, we often do not think about the emotions we ought to foster, in ourselves and others, to facilitate problem-solving. Schools often leave us with the impression that we can solve any problem through careful analysis alone. That is not true. Even the most careful analysis will not resolve a dispute if the relationship is charged with hostile emotions.

To make a working relationship effective, we would like to replace those emotions that tend to have a negative impact on our ability to deal with differences with emotions that are likely to have a constructive impact. A first step toward doing this is to recognize such emotional states.

Emotions	
likely to have a distorting impact	**likely to have a constructive impact**
in oneself	
insecurity	security
hopelessness	optimism
helplessness	confidence
toward the other side	
rejection	acceptance
hostility	respect
infatuation	concern

Once we recognize possible weaknesses in our own emotional state and that of others, we can do things to enlist helpful emotions.

One way to instill a constructive emotional state in ourselves is to recall a time, place, and circumstance when our morale was high, when we were particularly optimistic, successful, and committed — and then mentally step back into that situation and recall the feelings and attitude we had. Despite a natural skepticism, we can start behaving now *as if* we were still motivated and inspired by those feelings. One friend, a skiing enthusiast, uses this technique. Whenever he wants to summon up feelings of exhilaration, skillfulness, and total concentration, he will mentally place himself on a ski slope and feel what it is like to be racing down. In such a way we can sometimes step out of one set of feelings and into another.

A second technique is to focus on the emotional state that we would like to have in our partner — the other party to the relationship — and adopt it for ourselves. Others are more likely to show concern for us if we show concern for them, to acknowledge their emotions if we acknowledge ours, to be optimistic if we show optimism. This technique is unconditionally constructive. It doesn't cost us anything, and whether or not our partner follows suit, the process of trying to help the other person develop constructive feelings is likely to help us.

A more general guideline is to be aware of the emotional needs of others and to consider taking actions that might enhance in them an emotional state that would improve our joint ability to deal with differences. If others are feeling insecure, we may be able to take steps that will increase their security. For example, an employee may be working at far below his optimal level of performance because he is afraid he may fail in a new job. He may be covering up mistakes, working too slowly to make sure he does things right, or failing to contribute to discussions because he is afraid of looking stupid. These are signs of a poor working relationship between employer and employee. An alert manager will note this behavior, diagnose the problem as emotional insecurity, and take steps to deal with it. If the employee's job is in fact secure and his opinions respected, the manager will assure him to that effect.

All in all, the injunction to be rational is not a prescription to reject emotions, or to ignore or suppress them, but rather to think about them, exercise self-control over how we express them, and enlist them. In any relationship, being honest about emotions, discussing them candidly, and dealing with them jointly will enhance an ability to deal with conflicts and problems — rational and emotional — that are bound to occur. Preserving a balance between emotion and reason is unconditionally constructive. It helps the working relationship, and it helps me whether or not my relationship partners follow the same policy. And it is even better for me if they do.

5 Understanding

Learn how they see things

EVEN IF I take a rational look at a problem in my relationship with you, I may not be able to solve it because I may not fully understand it. The problem itself may exist only because of a misunderstanding. I may think you have eaten the last piece of pumpkin pie when, in fact, there is another piece in the refrigerator. Or we may have a real conflict that I fail to appreciate because I do not understand what you want or how you see things in general. For example, I may unwittingly schedule a meeting for the day of Yom Kippur, a holiday that you will be observing. Until I understand how you see things, it will not be easy for us to work out our differences.

Conversely, the greater the extent to which we comprehend each other's perceptions, concerns, and values — both in general and in particular — the greater our ability to work together. Other things being equal, the better the mutual understanding, the better the working relationship. And we can improve our understanding if at least one of us takes an unconditionally constructive approach to doing so.

We can't solve differences without understanding them

Misunderstandings so commonly contribute to ongoing problems, and to an inability to solve them, that "we have a misunderstanding" and "we have a problem" have become nearly synonymous. If asked why their marriage or friendship fell apart, two people might well say, "We didn't understand each other anymore" or "We didn't see things the same way."

In some cases, our understanding of a situation creates a problem in our heads that is not there in reality. A friend recently recalled how bad he felt when he had misunderstood his three-year-old son. The son had been picking at his dinner and getting down from his chair to play with his toys. The father, reading the paper in another room, told his son to sit back down and eat. A minute later, the child walked out of the kitchen and came up to his father. His father looked into the kitchen, saw food still on the plate, spanked the child, and sent him back into the kitchen. In fact, the boy had put a large bite of food into his mouth and was coming to show his father how much he was eating.

History is filled with simple misunderstandings that damaged an international relationship. In 1962, General Secretary Nikita Khrushchev, addressing the United Nations in New York, made a now infamous speech. Pounding a shoe on the podium, he proclaimed, "We will bury" the Western capitalist countries. Most Americans interpreted this as a threat, a statement that the goal of the Soviet Union was to bomb the United States into oblivion. After the U.S. press widely reported the "threatening" language, scholars and Soviet officials pointed out that in Russian the phrase did not imply a threat, but simply expressed the belief that the Soviet system would outlive the Western system. A healthy young Russian might easily say, "I will bury my father," meaning, "I expect to be around after he is gone." Nevertheless, some Americans still refer to the speech as a belligerent Soviet threat. That misunderstanding contributed to the difficulty our two countries have in dealing with our differences.

In contrast, each of us can feel the ease of working with someone who understands our concerns and perceptions. It is a sign of a good working relationship when a man greets his wife at the end of the day: "When we spoke on the phone this afternoon, I could tell from the sound of your voice that you were having a bad day. I canceled my five o'clock meeting so that I could come home and make dinner. And I told George not to come over tonight to watch the football game." When we understand each other, we can anticipate potential problems and prevent them from occurring.

If relationships stumble because of a lack of understanding, what are the barriers to better understanding, and how can they be overcome?

Misunderstandings arise for many reasons: I misspoke, you misheard; I had old data while you had the latest information, and so on. To the extent that these are problems of communication, the next chapter suggests ways to ensure that our communications are clear and effective.

Other barriers to understanding that each of us can affect are:

- we may not realize how little we understand;
- we may fear learning that we are "wrong"; and
- we may not know how to develop better understanding.

For each of these barriers, there are remedies that we can pursue unconditionally, whether or not others do.

**Explore their thinking;
we may not know how little we know**

If you and I have difficulty in dealing with our differences, I may not be aware of how you see things — and of the importance of understanding how you see things. The less I know, the more likely I am to underestimate how little I know. Like a city I have never visited, the inside of someone else's mind is terra incognita. It is so unknown that I am unlikely to appreciate how unknown it is.

Nor am I likely to appreciate how important it is to our relationship for me to explore that territory and learn what I can about it. If, for example, I notice that during the summer my secretary sometimes comes to work late or takes a day's leave on short notice, I may become upset, treat her coldly, and, when she does come in, give her extra work to make up for lost time. As a result, she may eventually quit. But if, instead, I tried to understand her situation, I might learn that she is a single parent with three young children who do not go to school in the summer; that she drives them thirty miles to her mother's house every morning before work; and that her mother has been ill recently and unable to take the children. And I might discover that she would be happy to stay until 6:00 or 7:00 P.M., if only she could come in at 10:00 or 11:00 A.M.

The more foreign the other side in a relationship, the less likely we are to know what is important to them. Unaware of our own ignorance, it is only with hindsight that we may learn of it. Where there are differences of language, custom, and culture, it requires imagination and effort to identify potential problems. When U.S. companies have entered foreign markets, they have often made mistakes because they did not understand the local culture. In a stark example of misunderstanding, General Motors introduced its

Chevrolet Nova into Spanish-speaking markets without realizing that, in Spanish, *no va* means "don't go."

Even when companies try to anticipate conflicts, they may find themselves conducting business in a manner that causes conflicts in the foreign business community. The Gillette Company thoroughly researched the economics of the Japanese market before it introduced its razor blades into Japan, but it failed to understand Japanese business customs. As a result, Gillette tended to treat its Japanese distributors as if they were U.S. distributors. If a distributor did not meet Gillette's standards, it was dropped and replaced. In Japan, where loyalty and the cultivation of long-term relationships are important, Gillette's approach offended both distributors and customers. Schick better understood the local practice, cultivated a stable relationship with one distributor, and currently dominates the razor blade market in Japan.

One reason we may fail to make an effort to find out about the people with whom we are dealing is because we think we know all we need to know. Another is that we have an unduly narrow view of the kind of information that is relevant to us. Some business managers, for example, think they can manage a business just as they invest in the stock market — strictly by the numbers. The attitude may be, "If we want a working relationship, let's get to work. None of this 'touchy feely' stuff. I don't need to know you well. I make deals with strangers over the telephone. All I need to know is your phone number, your credit card number, and a few basic facts."

It is true that we want the problem-solving aspect of a relationship for utilitarian reasons and that to understand someone takes time. And less effort may be justified in a one-time encounter than in an ongoing relationship. But in both cases, an investment in understanding usually pays off. As we increase our level of understanding, our ability to avoid some problems and resolve others will improve and become more consistent.

Always assume a need to learn more. If I want to improve our ability to deal with differences, I should *always* assume that I do not understand enough. I should always explore for more. It is easy for me to believe that *you* need to know more; much harder to recognize that *I* do. But by acknowledging my ignorance, I open myself to learning and encourage you to do the same.

A retired executive recounted a good example of the need for exploration. The executive, Paul Kramer, had for years been managing a division of one company that was sold to another. The new owners retained Kramer to run the business, but placed him under a new group vice-president. The group vice-president and his staff had analyzed the division before the purchase and thought they knew how to improve its performance. They sent down directives to change the pricing, eliminate small customers, and drop unprofitable product lines. Kramer believed he knew the business well. He strongly objected to the new directives, but he did not make a detailed study of the analyses on which they were based. After a bitter confrontation, the new policies were implemented, Kramer resigned, and business slipped away.

Kramer and the new group vice-president each knew a great deal — and each thought he knew enough. In hindsight, Kramer admitted that he could have learned something from the pricing and market analyses that the new owners had made. And they, he knew, had much to learn from his years of experience. Either Kramer or the new group vice-president could probably have avoided the problem by being less confident that he knew enough and by actively exploring the knowledge and ideas of the other.

In such cases, acknowledging a lack of understanding is

not enough. I need to make an effort to learn more — a vigorous search to enhance my understanding of you. And by actively exploring your concerns, I encourage you to be curious about mine. More than two thousand years ago, the Latin writer Publilius Syrus noted, "We are interested in others when they are interested in us."

Start by asking, "What do they care about?" Even when we are aware of our ignorance and open to new ideas, the problem of trying to understand others may overwhelm us. We often do not understand even our closest friends. If we had to understand everything about everyone with whom we have a relationship, we would have time for little else. Part of our reluctance to try to understand another person may come from a hesitancy to start a process without limits. I can solve this problem by limiting my attention to what is most important to solving problems: What are your interests in this situation, what are your perceptions of me and the problem, and what underlying values of yours may be at stake?

Interests. A good solution to a particular problem should meet your interests as well as mine. A good place to start in improving my understanding of you, both in general and for the purpose of dealing with differences, is to explore your interests. The better I understand your interests — your concerns, your needs, your wants, your hopes, and your fears — the better the chance that we will be able to satisfy them, at least minimally.

If, for example, I am your boss, I should try to understand your interests as an employee. Do you want more responsibility or less? More job security or more opportunity for growth? A more flexible work schedule or a more predictable one? More feedback or more independence? More income now or in the future? A one-year job or a lifetime career? I will increase the chance of our finding an outcome satisfactory to both of us if I explore a wide range of your possible concerns rather than focusing narrowly on one particular difference, such as over salary.

Perceptions. When two people look at a problem, they rarely see it the same way. If I am going to deal with a problem that exists between us, I need to understand how *you* see it. Not only our differences, but the chance to resolve them successfully, may depend on our differing perceptions.

Suppose, in discussing our differences about your salary, I learn that to your way of thinking 8:00 A.M. is a normal starting time for a day's work (in contrast to my view that the working day doesn't really start until about 9:30), and that a normal "eight-hour day" is 8:00 A.M. to 5:00 P.M. with an hour for lunch. This difference in perception might lead to a solution in which, in addition to whatever other raise was appropriate, you got an extra 10 percent or so for working an hour more per day than others in the office.

It is not enough simply to know intellectually that others have different perceptions — that they have some "odd" ways of looking at things — because that is not how their perceptions seem to them. To work with others successfully, I should understand how they reasonably came to hold their views and how it feels to be a person with those views. Look again at the charts of U.S.-Soviet partisan perceptions in Chapter 3. In most situations, a good test of our understanding of another's perception is the ability to write out such a chart so that an impartial reader finds both columns persuasive.

Values. Underlying the particular interests and perceptions of a person in a given situation are more basic values. These may include qualities like loyalty, team spirit, security, honesty, bravery, pride of workmanship, and family cohesiveness. One way I can learn something about your values is to rank your interests in order of their importance to you. Continuing with the example of our salary negotiation, I may discover that much as you like money, you really care more about your title and not having to worry about layoffs. Working together to understand values that are important to you — perhaps status and security — we can then look for a solution that you will value highly. I might offer you the title of Department Director, for example, and guarantee you a position for at least three years. While I may pay you less than I pay others, and thus conserve my budget, you may still find this proposal fair and reasonable.

Understanding the values of a relationship partner is even more important if two cultures are involved. In working with Japanese business people, it can be surprising to hear them describe the American value system as it sometimes appears to them: "Why does American business place such little value on loyalty?" When asked to explain, the Japanese cite examples of Americans leaving the company that trained them to take a job with a competitor, and of companies changing suppliers to obtain a slightly lower price. "And why does American management place so little value on corporate responsibility?" — here pointing to a company president who denies personal fault rather than accept responsibility for the company's mistakes. (In contrast, when a Japan Air Lines jumbo jet crashed because of a faulty rear bulkhead, the president of the company immediately resigned and undertook to apologize personally to the families of each of the dead.) Yet U.S. business leaders look at the Japanese system and ask why the Japanese place so little value on the free market system and instead subsidize Japanese companies and erect barriers to imports.

Both Japanese and U.S. business people are reasonable.

Neither value system is immoral or "wrong." But it is difficult for partners from the two countries to work together unless they understand the values of the other.

Knowledge of the interests, perceptions, and values of others does not come easily, and we can never know them completely. But we will more quickly and effectively build the kind of understanding that will improve a working relationship if we understand their interests and the perceptions and values that affect them. We can and should take steps to do so, unconditionally, whether or not they reciprocate.

Don't be afraid to learn something new

If I am trying to build a better relationship with someone I already know — particularly someone with whom I now have a confrontational relationship — coming to understand the way he or she sees things will usually require me to *unlearn* some preconceptions. The labor relations personnel for a company with a history of union strikes, for example, will have some impression of the union leadership — an impression that is no doubt partially valid. But as they come to understand the union leaders better, they will probably find that they must abandon some of their old perceptions.

Unlearning can be uncomfortable. As I change my views, I may have to question some of my past decisions, and others — I may fear — will question my wisdom. This process is especially uncomfortable when it concerns ideas we hold strongly. We are emotionally committed to these beliefs, and we tend to avoid or ignore information that would contradict them. Sometimes our fear of listening and learning may stem from the fear that if we did learn more, we would discover that we had made mistakes in the past.

When we learn, we may feel discomfort for two reasons. First, we may be afraid of losing face, of looking stupid to others. The more publicly we have committed ourselves to a certain way of looking at things, the more important this source of discomfort will be. Second, we may feel uncomfortable because we are psychologically insecure. This may be the same kind of discomfort we feel about going to see a psychiatrist. We might learn something that would force us to rearrange our ideas, both about ourselves and others. This process may be uncomfortable even if no one else is aware of it.

In the seventeenth century, the astronomer Galileo published papers proposing that the earth was not the center of the universe and that the planets revolved around the sun. These propositions contradicted the teachings of the Catholic Church, which asserted as an article of faith that the earth was the center of the universe. But Galileo's propositions were not new. Copernicus, a Polish astronomer and theologian, had suggested similar ideas a hundred years before, and by the seventeenth century many scholars believed that the sun was the center of the solar system. Yet the Church submitted Galileo to the Inquisition, forced him to recant his beliefs, and confined him to his home for the rest of his life. It was many years before the Church leadership would change its teachings and admit its mistake.

Especially in adversarial international relationships, rather than welcoming a better understanding of an opponent's point of view, we tend to fear or reject it as likely to weaken our resolve. During a discussion with U.S. military officers during the Vietnam War, a U.S. Army colonel explained why he did not try to understand the North Vietnamese view of the war: "If we were to understand how they see it, it would weaken our will to fight." The weaker our confidence in our own views, the more defensive we are likely to be about them and the less interested in understanding conflicting views. Fearing that if we understood a situation differently we might have to act differently, we may deny ourselves an understanding that might help us devise better solutions than we can now contemplate.

Be open and confident. One way to reduce the risk of being proven wrong is to avoid early commitments and remain open to new information. A union leader who says, "We will consider every opportunity to avoid a strike, and we are always open to new ideas from management," will have more flexibility to negotiate good agreements and take advantage of management concessions than one who says, even implicitly, "We have decided to strike, and nothing you can say will change our minds."

Even when we announce a decision or make a commitment, we can leave the door open.

> No, Terry, even though you feel broke, and even though your college expenses seem higher than you expected, your mother and I have decided not to increase your monthly allowance, at least for now. If you will keep records for a month of where your money goes and come in with a budget for the balance of the college year, we are prepared to consider an increase measured by a reasonable estimate of your needs, but not one based on what you want or what the Millers are giving Jonathan.

In this way we can rule out unsatisfactory options without closing off all discussion. And we leave ourselves open to a new view without any loss of face in the light of new information.

If what we fear in learning that we have been wrong is loss of *self*-respect, then we need a different standard by which to judge ourselves. Rather than assuming that we have nothing to learn, we might base our self-esteem on how *well* we learn. How easily do we absorb new information? How quickly do we spot mistaken assumptions? How comfortable can we be in acknowledging error?

The more we understand our true interests, our options, our strengths, and our weaknesses, the more open we can be to new ideas without fear or discomfort. When we are open to persuasion, we demonstrate our ability to deal well with changing circumstances. General Secretary Mikhail Gorbachev undoubtedly views his policy of *glasnost,* or openness, as a sign of strength. He appears willing to accept the West and learn from it. Thus he appears stronger than his predecessors, who hid behind secrecy and assumed they had nothing to learn from Western society. Acting according to our convictions is a sign of strength, but being open to changing our convictions — when justified on the merits — is a sign of even greater strength.

Use tools to break into their world

We respond to events in ways that reflect our own concerns and values. Even if I learn something about the way you see things, I am likely to consider your concerns as less important and less urgent than mine.

One reason businesses hire outside consultants is because it is easier for an outsider to evaluate objectively the strengths and potential of a company than it is for those within. When a manager from one division is promoted to the top of a company, he tends to favor his old division. If the manager is astute, he will know that he does not see the overall picture objectively. He will also know that it is difficult for him to set aside his long experience and take a fresh view, so a consultant may help.

It is a common mistake in every kind of relationship to

assume that our concerns and priorities are shared by others. The vigor with which El Salvador embraced the Central American peace initiative (the "Arias Plan") in August 1987 surprised many U.S. officials. After supporting the U.S.-backed contra forces for so long, the Salvadoran government suddenly seemed ready to stop all support and allow the Nicaraguan government to survive. To the United States, the threat of a Marxist-Leninist government in Nicaragua was the primary concern, and the new peace plan did not solve that issue. But to the Salvadorans, the primary issue was Nicaraguan support for the Salvadoran rebels. They cared less that Nicaragua might remain Marxist. Many officials in the United States, concerned foremost with the rebellion in Nicaragua, did not understand that the Salvadorans would readily accept a proposal that could end Nicaraguan support for the insurgency in El Salvador.

A poor understanding of others is a natural outcome of our self-centered view of the world. If we hope to improve our understanding and consequently our ability to solve problems with others, we will need to find ways to step outside ourselves — to understand the world from other points of view. Some specific techniques or tools can help us do that.

Learn their story. Think of the current situation or problem as the result of two stories — mine and yours. I know mine, but probably do not know yours. What has happened to you? How did you get here?

A story should cover the events that brought another person into a relationship with me. And it should include a "plot" — the connections that brought these events together. A story may be the account of someone's life or what happened to that person today that led up to an accident. Learning someone else's story helps overcome my self-centeredness and reveals facts, perceptions, and values that I would otherwise miss. Also, the better I know someone's story, the more likely that person is to become someone of concern to me. That concern will itself help us work through our problems.

Reverse roles. Try to imagine the other person's situation and assume their role. It helps to be as explicit as possible. If I am trying to understand my boss, I should imagine how it *feels* to sit in his office on the thirty-fourth floor, to go to the regular Monday morning management committee meeting where *his* boss, the president, grills him about the performance of his division; to be fifty-six years old with little chance to advance to the top spot; to have three children in college; and so forth.

With practice, we can more easily understand contrary points of view. Foreign service officers can enhance their ability to understand other governments by altering the way they read news accounts or diplomatic reports about them. They can imagine themselves as the foreigner who wrote the speech or delivered it, or as the person described in the dispatch, and ask themselves:

> How would I have to think in order to be comfortable doing or saying those things and at the same time consider myself a good person, pursuing laudable ends by means that are justified under the circumstances?

Not all foreign officials sees themselves as good people, but the chance of our coming to understand others is far greater if we assume that others see themselves favorably rather than as bad people, pursuing immoral ends through illegitimate means.

Draft a chart of their currently perceived choice. When we want to understand the other side's interests, perceptions, and values, it may not be clear how to start or what's important. Focusing on a specific choice they face can help.

In my ongoing relationship with you, I am likely to have an unresolved issue. I can develop a chart that gives me some insight into how you may think about that issue by considering a choice you face, as you may see it, and then listing the consequences, again as you probably see them, of your deciding one way or the other. My objective is a chart that will illuminate your interests, values, and important perceptions. It may help if I think about what concerns I might have if I were in your circumstances and had to make the same choice.

Suppose you are an important customer of mine, and I want to convince you to make my company, Solutions, Inc., your exclusive supplier of computers. I would also like to improve our working relationship. So far, however, while you have been cordial, you have not shown much enthusiasm for an exclusive contract. To understand your thinking better, I can try to work out a chart such as the one on the following page. If it represents a good approximation of your thinking, then I will understand how this particular decision looks within your web of concerns and interests.

Having produced this chart, I will understand that if I want to improve the chance that you will accept me as an exclusive supplier, I will have to change the way you see your choice. Perhaps I can offer to contract the service to a larger company, guarantee prices below a certain benchmark, offer to diversify the risk by subcontracting to other companies, and enhance your image in your company by helping you prepare a presentation showing how much money this contract would save. Or perhaps I will conclude that I should change the question and ask only to be your lead supplier.

Customer's Currently Perceived Choice

QUESTION:
Shall I make Solutions, Inc., our exclusive supplier
for computers?

Consequences if I do	Consequences if I don't
− I won't have the option of calling on several companies for service.	+ I can call on two or three suppliers to support my machines.
− Solutions may increase the price on me after it gets the exclusive.	+ I can keep competitive pressure on prices.
− Solutions might go bankrupt; all my eggs are in one basket.	+ I diversify my risk by spreading my purchases among several suppliers.
− If something goes wrong with our deal, my boss will blame me.	+ I can always defend myself by saying I diversified the risk.
+ Solutions might give me a volume discount.	+ I keep my options open.
	− I might not be able to get as large a discount.

No chart like this will guarantee that I understand your thinking. And in order to construct one, I need to have some understanding of the situation. But building such a chart does give me a systematic way to organize my thinking. It provides good questions for further exploration. By going back and forth between what I know and what I can guess, I can see how the pieces fit together. I can come to understand how you can feel that what you are doing is reasonable. I improve my understanding of both your immediate concerns and of the perceptions and deeper values that underlie them.

Once I have something on paper, I can use it to check my assumptions with knowledgeable third parties or directly with you. Using such a chart in this way can help me learn more while showing you that I am trying to understand your point of view.

Use a third party. In many situations, we will find it difficult to put ourselves in another person's shoes. We may not have time, we may be plagued with pressures that require our attention, or we may have such strong views that we cannot break outside ourselves. If so, it may be useful to ask the help of a third party.

In the construction industry, for instance, businesses that have an ongoing working relationship often end up in litigation. In such situations, settling a dispute quickly and fairly may be far more important than the precise terms of any settlement. Mediation can help each company better understand the perceptions of the other. Similarly, in family relations, a therapist can often help family members break out of a destructive pattern of interaction by helping each better understand how the world looks through the eyes of the other. Outside help for improving understanding is most important when feelings run high.

In competitive or antagonistic situations, a company or government can improve its understanding of the other side by assigning one or more people to advocate its interests in internal discussions. A need for such a mechanism may exist where officials within a company or government see it as risky to oppose the desires or beliefs of their superiors.

For a U.S. official to advance ideas that appear empathetic toward the Soviet point of view might seem disloyal, especially during a crisis when tensions are high. Yet it is during such periods, like the Cuban missile crisis of October 1962 or the October 1973 Middle East war, when a full understanding is most important. An institutional mechanism can overcome the natural but dangerous pressure toward "groupthink."

The Catholic Church long ago established the role of devil's advocate to urge the case against the canonization of a saint. Without such an established and legitimate role, few within the Church might wish to speak ill of someone nominated for sainthood.

It was widely reported that during the Vietnam War, Undersecretary of State George Ball took on the role of presenting the case against various military proposals being considered. The semi-institutionalization of that role was undoubtedly a good idea, because it reduced the political cost of appearing to differ with the president.

Our legal system bases the right to representation by a lawyer on a similar principle. The courts have noted that the right to representation is most important when public opinion is most strongly opposed to a criminal defendant. In these cases, an advocate who will help the court understand the defendant's position is critical to a fair decision. The right to representation is so well established that no one (well, almost no one) blames a lawyer for vigorously advocating the case of an unpopular client.

We can improve upon the role of an advocate for the other side by placing someone in the role of "the other side." It would be the job of such a person to act like an official in the other government, helping us understand how he and his colleagues might view a situation and how that view might be reasonable.

In war games and crisis simulations, a few officials in the U.S. government are asked to play the role of Soviets. News reports indicate that they tend to put themselves into the role, defined not as Soviets would define themselves, but as wearing the black hats of an "enemy" that would fit the definition of the worst possible Communist villain. In preparing military plans for all contingencies, that is one possibility we should consider. But it is unlikely that the Soviets see themselves that way. To gain a more accurate understanding of what the Soviets might really do in these situations, the U.S. government should look for more probable Soviet perceptions of themselves. We might, for example, have a small working group construct visions of Soviet perceptions, interests, and values — visions that empathetically portray the Soviet point of view in a way that Soviets would accept.

In summary, we can overcome the common barriers to better understanding in our working relationships by pursuing three unconditionally constructive steps: explore their thinking, be open to learning, and use tools to break into their world. Each of these steps can be undertaken unconditionally without concern that the other side will gain or benefit from our unilateral action. Every effort we make to understand those with whom we deal is good for us, and good for the relationship, whether or not they follow suit.

6 | Communication

Always consult before deciding — and listen

To HAVE A working relationship, we have to communicate. What we communicate and how we do it — whether with a friend, a spouse, an employer, or a government — affect our ability to deal with differences. Poor communication can lead to misunderstanding, unhelpful emotions, distrust, sloppy thinking, and poor outcomes.

Communication is a broad field. It has many aspects beyond those involved in developing a working relationship. This chapter focuses on three barriers to good communication and some unconditionally constructive strategies that anyone in a relationship can use to improve communication in ways that help solve problems.

Many people measure the quality of a relationship by the quality of the communication. "We don't talk" means that the relationship has broken down, while "we talk about everything" means the relationship is healthy. The way we communicate reveals the nature of a relationship. Just the tone of voice used by a parent to a child, one spouse to another, or a superior to a subordinate tells us much about how they deal with each other. A hostile tone, interruptions, and shouting indicate a relationship that is likely to foster more problems than it can solve. A short telegram, an aide-mémoire, or an impersonal business letter may convey more by its form than its content.

Good communication need not indicate friendship. Communicating effectively with those with whom we have fundamental disagreements is more difficult but often more important than communicating with those we like. The United States and Soviet governments recognize their interest in maintaining communication *especially* when disagreements are most serious. In 1987, the two governments agreed to upgrade the "hot line" between their capitals and establish crisis communication centers so that their communication will be most direct when it's most needed.

Communication is complex. We communicate with every movement and action, often without conscious intent. Silence itself can send a powerful signal. It may mean, "I am upset, don't bother me," or "I am thinking hard about what you just said." Body position and movement may convey warm openness or cold rejection.

The emotional impact of my communication may determine whether someone will *want* to work with me. All of us have had the experience of meeting someone for the first time and feeling an instant rapport. After a few brief words, I understand what you are trying to say and you seem to understand me precisely. I am comfortable with you and enjoy your company. There is a mutual rhythm in the conversation and both of us are fully engaged.

If we are communicating poorly, on the other hand, the symptoms may be equally clear. I am uncomfortable and ill at ease. When I am talking, you look away. You appear to assume that you know all you need to know about me and do not care to learn more. There are uncomfortable pauses in the conversation, forced laughs at jokes that are not funny. Neither of us learns anything from the conversation;

neither listens. Unless I can do something to change the way we are communicating, I am likely to leave such a conversation feeling frustrated and unproductive. I will want to avoid you in the future. The feeling will be mutual.

Each communication helps establish a pattern of interaction that plays a crucial role in the ability to deal with future problems. A mother who yells at her daughter may see an immediate response, but may find that she has created a barrier between herself and her child as that daughter grows older. Any message that cuts off future communication handicaps both sides.

Poor communication can hurt every element of a good working relationship. What prevents our communicating in ways that help us deal with differences?

THREE BARRIERS
TO EFFECTIVE
COMMUNICATION

Communications go awry in many ways and for many reasons. Some are beyond our control. But there are others each of us can affect with modest effort and no risk:

- We assume there is no need to talk.
- We communicate in one direction: we "tell" people.
- We send mixed messages.

1. We assume there is no need to talk.

Perhaps the most important explanation for failed communication in a relationship is the common assumption that there is no reason to discuss a particular matter. A husband, for example, without consulting his wife, may have made a decision that affects her. He may have done so because:

- it didn't occur to him to talk with her about it;
- his mind was focused on the substance of the matter;
- he thought he knew what the right decision was;
- he thought he knew what she would say; or
- in the last analysis, the decision was one he himself would have to make.

His wife may have had an interest in the decision, known things that would have led him to decide otherwise, or had views quite different from those he imagined. His decision may have been a mistake. But even if he made the right decision and correctly guessed what she would say, the process was unwise. The husband may have surprised his wife, thereby appearing a little less reliable in her eyes. He confronted her with a fait accompli, tending to make her feel coerced, not persuaded. And by unilaterally deciding something that affects her, he sent the implicit message that she, her interests, and her views were not worthy of consideration — a view exactly contrary to the kind of acceptance that helps build a working relationship.

Government officials can also assume that there is no need to talk. In 1985, U.S. Secretary of State George P. Shultz skipped a meeting of foreign ministers to protest New Zealand's decision to bar U.S. nuclear-armed warships from New Zealand ports. David Lange, then both prime minister and foreign minister of New Zealand, was certainly correct when, without insisting that New Zealand's policy was sound, he did insist that reducing communication was no way to solve the problem: "the important point about a longstanding alliance is that the members must be able to talk out their differences" (*New York Times,* March 5, 1985, p. A3).

2. We communicate in one direction: we "tell" people.

Even when we do see the need to communicate, we often assume that it simply means telling something to somebody else. For communication to be effective, it needs to be two-way: there must be not only transmission, but reception. Listening is essential.

We may talk so much that we discourage the other side from listening. Consider the case of a couple in which the husband is talkative and the wife quiet. If an observer were to interrupt the husband's flow of words at some point and ask the wife what he had been saying, the answer might be, "I have no idea." One way to adapt to an extremely talkative person is to stop listening. Why listen? There is no interchange. Building a relationship with such a person is as difficult as building one with a loudspeaker.

If both relationship partners talk but one ignores the other, the communication is still one-way. In the 1950s, General Electric dealt with its largest labor union by presenting its contract proposals on a take-it-or-leave-it basis. Although General Electric's proposals were fair enough to be accepted by the workers, and although it occasionally made modest changes, it tried by publicizing an unbending firmness to make itself unable to alter a position once taken. The union sued. The courts sided with the union, ruling that good faith bargaining requires one to be open to change — requires genuine listening as well as talking.

The consequences of one-way communication can be as bad as those of none at all. Like the husband who failed to consult his wife, if we communicate solely by transmitting our opinions, we cut off the chance to learn things we don't know and discourage the other side from contributing to a solution. Further, we reduce their commitment to any solution.

3. We send mixed messages

To be effective, communication should be consistent: what I say today should agree with what I said yesterday and what I will say tomorrow. What you heard me telling someone else should fit with what I told you. My words should be consistent with each other and with my actions. Mixed messages undermine each other and prevent effective communication.

Inconsistency is particularly damaging to our ability to build a working relationship. On a personal level, we feel uneasy with someone who gives lip service to one way of living and acts differently. We get mixed messages from the fundamentalist evangelist who has an affair with a secretary and defrauds the church. Some people may succeed in ignoring one message or the other, but most will find the conflict disturbing: something does not ring true. The Soviet Union preaches noninterference while it has a hundred thousand troops in Afghanistan. The United States preaches "no ransom for hostages" while negotiating an arms-for-hostages deal with Iran. When we hear such conflicting messages, we become skeptical and confused, not only about the speaker's interests, but also about his or her reliability; we do not know which message, if either, to believe. As a result, future joint problem-solving will be more difficult.

Mixed messages are common in our communication for three reasons: we communicate about mixed interests; we address ourselves to multiple audiences; and our mixed emotions may send out confusing signals.

Mixed purposes. One of my goals may be to improve a working relationship, but I always have a number of other goals as well. Because my short- and long-term interests often conflict, an explicit message I transmit to further one set of interests may contain implicit messages that conflict with the other set. Long-term concerns are drowned out by short-term goals that seem — at the moment — more urgent. If I tell my young daughter, "I'm busy; please don't bother me," hoping to finish an urgent piece of work, she may hear a far more general message that I am not interested in her. That second, implicit message might have been avoided if, aware of the problem, I had added, "Could you come back in twenty minutes with a book you'd like me to read to you?"

A message we send one day in pursuit of one goal may be inconsistent with one we send the next day, when we have a different interest in mind. If I angrily rebuke a supplier for missing a deadline, hoping that he won't miss another, he may hear that I want to change suppliers. And he may pay no attention to my later comment about wanting an ongoing business relationship.

Multiple audiences. We often want to say different things to different audiences, for reasons that are perfectly legitimate. The CEO of a publicly held corporation faces this situation when writing an annual report, which must satisfy several constituencies: shareholders, employees, and investment analysts. To each, the CEO may wish to emphasize different points. If the report says the company expects to reduce labor costs in the coming year, the shareholders may be pleased, but the employees upset. To improve the company's ability to work with each, the CEO will have to choose his words carefully.

Mixed emotions. Suppose I tell my staff that they can interrupt me at any time to voice strong concerns about the office. The week after I announce this policy, however, I have a run-in with my boss that upsets and angers me. If my assistants come in that morning to tell me they are unhappy with the vacation schedule, I may show irritation and anger even as I try to listen to them. I may still say, "Thank you for bringing this to my attention. You can do so any time," but they will get a quite different message, one that says, "Don't bother me when I have something else on my mind."

Other emotions can further confuse messages. Anxiety on my part, or a desire not to upset you, may lead me to "beat around the bush," to avoid communicating clearly in a way that will be easily understood. This indirect approach can cause problems. An employee who is afraid to ask for a day off may raise the subject with the boss by commenting on how many days off others have taken. If the rapport between the two is excellent, the boss may understand, but otherwise he may think the employee is whining and trying to make others look bad.

Emotions play a large role in determining not only what we say and how we say it but what we hear. If I am upset, angry, or frightened, I will interpret what you say in the light of my emotional state. An innocuous statement of fact — such as "I'll be talking with your boss tomorrow" — may be interpreted as a threat. A silence may appear highly suspicious. A failure to return a phone call may seem proof of personal rejection.

THREE WAYS TO
STRENGTHEN THE RELATIONSHIP

To overcome these barriers to an effective problem-solving relationship, we need both a general strategy and some specific techniques to deal with particular communications problems. The suggested general strategy has three components:

1. Always consult before deciding.
2. Listen actively.
3. Plan the process.

1. ACBD: Always Consult Before Deciding

As a general rule, if you and I have an ongoing relationship and I would like to improve our ability to deal with differences, then I should consult you before making a decision that would significantly affect you. To consult means to ask your advice. It is not enough to tell you a decision after it has been made. Consultation does not require that we agree or that I give up such authority as I may have to make a decision. But it does require that I inform you of a matter on which I may decide, that I request your advice and views and listen to them, and that I take them into account in making a decision.

For instance, the president of a company is facing her third straight quarter of losses. She believes she must reduce the payroll, but she has to worry about a union. She might invite the union leaders to her office, explain the reasons for the cutback, and say something along the following lines:

> Ultimately, it is my responsibility to the company and its shareholders to decide how best to reduce our payroll. But before I make any decision, I'd like to learn your views of the employees' interests and how you think they might be affected by various options. I would also like to hear any ideas you may have on how our production could be restructured to make it more competitive. We want to be expanding, not contracting. I can't promise to implement your suggestions, but I'll certainly consider them and use them if I think they'll help.

Consultation of this kind should be the norm of every working relationship. It should take place whether I am making plans for next weekend (I should consult my spouse) or the U.S. government is making plans to send a fleet to the Persian Gulf (it should consult allies and friendly governments in the area).

We cannot adopt a rigid rule to consult relationship partners before making any decision that may affect them. Some circumstances will require quick decisions. In other cases, a decision may affect so many people (perhaps every employee in a factory or every citizen in a city) that advance consultation with each one is out of the question. Perhaps the impact of our decision on someone will be slight. Or perhaps there is a risk that disclosure of a proposed decision will generate opposition that will cause serious problems for both of us. This consultation guideline, like others, is subject to reasonable exceptions.

Nonetheless, the practice of consulting relationship partners before making decisions that significantly affect them — whether they are family members or foreign governments — is unconditionally constructive. It will be good for the working relationship and good for me whether or not you follow the same practice. We can see this by examining how a practice of consulting before deciding improves each of the elements of a good working relationship.

Consult to help balance emotion with reason. We cannot avoid our emotions and those of others — nor should we try to. But we can often avoid the damaging impact that emotions can have on communication and that emotional communications, in turn, can have on a working relationship. A policy of consulting a relationship partner gives us time to think and reduces the risk of a hasty decision.

Consult to promote better understanding. If I routinely consult you before making any significant decision that will affect you, I will promote mutual understanding. I let you know what I am thinking of doing and why, and I ask for your concerns, ideas, and suggestions. I listen and take them into account. The process improves our understanding of each other's thinking.

Consult to promote two-way communication. The general guideline of consulting before deciding engages both parties in talking and listening. Consultation *is* two-way communication: I tell you of a situation, I ask your advice, and (if you are willing to give it) I receive it. One person can stimulate two-way communication. The best advice is to ask advice.

Consult to be more reliable. If, without advance notice, I make decisions that affect you, you will often be caught by surprise. The more often this happens, the less able you will be to predict my behavior and the less reliable I will appear in your eyes. You are likely to trust me less, not knowing what I am going to do next. If I ask your views before making a decision, you are less likely to be surprised and my behavior will tend to be more predictable. By simply giving advance notice — and doing what I tell you I am going to do — I can become more trustworthy.

Consult to avoid a coercive fait accompli. A unilateral decision by one that confronts the other with no chance to affect it will often feel coercive. Simply *informing* you before I take action may be enough to avoid damage to my reliability in your eyes. But to avoid your feeling coerced, I will need to *consult* you before making a decision and give you an opportunity to persuade me.

Consult to establish acceptance. The final element of a good working relationship is acceptance. If, without giving you an opportunity to help shape a decision, I decide the matter by myself, I am to that extent treating you as someone I will not deal with, whose interests and views deserve little consideration. Such behavior will prevent our having a good working relationship. If, on the other hand, I do consult you, I demonstrate that I am willing to deal with you and willing to consider your interests and views.

2. Listen actively

Sometimes in a relationship one of us is talking too much and listening too little. Perhaps, more commonly, neither of us — however much we are talking — is listening effectively to the other.

Find the listening needs and match them. The first step in active listening is to become aware of any listening problem. If you think you tend to dominate conversation, check yourself. Ask friends or colleagues to tell you if they observe you talking too much or not listening enough. Try recording the length of time you spend talking versus the length of time you spend listening.

Next, design an opportunity and setting that will be conducive to listening. Some marriage counselors, for example, advise their clients to make a "listening contract." The couple agrees to allow each spouse to talk without interruption for a period of time. Even without such ground rules, self-restraint will help. We sometimes talk every time we can think of something to say. If we are talking too much, a better rule is to talk only for a purpose, and to keep that purpose in mind.

Engage the other person. My active listening means more than sitting silently, although that is sometimes needed. It also means establishing conditions and asking questions that will draw you out and engage you. As we begin a conversation, I can use several techniques to establish personal rapport. I can adopt a manner that is harmonious with yours in terms of pace, volume and tone of voice, formality or informality, degree of relaxation, and so forth. We can sit more or less side by side with a pad of paper, chart, or other symbolic representation of "the problem" in front of us on which we can work jointly. And I can learn as much as possible about you in advance, so that my questions will reflect a genuine curiosity.

A variety of techniques can help me understand the specific content of what you wish to communicate. These include making short interjections that acknowledge points made, paraphrasing in my own language what I have heard to make sure that I have it right, taking short notes, maintaining intermittent eye contact, and asking follow-up questions. It can be particularly useful to repeat points that surprised me so that I will remember them instead of slipping back to a prior assumption. With careful listening, I will learn things that will help us improve our relationship in the future.

Inquire. No matter how sensitive I am when I listen, I will not be able to grasp fully what you are saying unless I understand something about you. Each of us may be transmitting ideas in our own jargon or conveying highlights that presume a common base of information that the other does not have. Just as understanding another person requires some communication, so communication requires some understanding of the other person's frame of reference and culture.

Nothing more dramatically illustrates the necessity of effective two-way communication than a cross-cultural relationship. When an anthropologist studies a primitive community, he may live there for several years, learning its language and customs, before he begins truly to understand what he is hearing and seeing. He knows that language is not enough. He will not understand the words or ways of the people until he understands the cultural context. We cannot know every culture. Yet the better we understand the culture and history of a foreign country, the more nearly we will come to understand their foreign policies and public statements.

We can measure our listening skills by asking ourselves how much we know about our relationship partners. Do we know how our friends feel about current political or social issues? about art? Do we know what is important in their lives? Do we know how our employees feel about their schedules or benefits? how the Mexican government feels about the new U.S. immigration law? If we draw blanks on questions like these, especially about matters on which we differ, we should probably be listening more carefully.

Speak clearly in ways that promote listening. If our communication is to be truly two-way, you will need to understand what I am trying to say. While I cannot force understanding on you, I can communicate in ways that make it more likely that you will understand me.

Speak for ourselves, not them. In general, we can speak in the first person, talking about what we have observed, what we think, and what we fear. And we can avoid putting words in their mouth, attributing motives to them, or telling them what they really think. "I'm feeling ignored" is likely to be more effective and constructive than "you're ignoring me."

Use short clear statements — and pause. With every statement I make, there is some risk, however small, that you will misinterpret what I mean. I may misspeak, use ambiguous words, forget critical points, use unfamiliar terms, and so on. The longer my statement, the greater the chance that one misinterpretation will confuse other points that I have tried to make. I can reduce that risk by avoiding long lectures, breaking complex messages into small parts, encouraging interchange, and allowing pauses so that each of us can digest what we have heard. If I have several important points, I can make them one at a time and give you an opportunity to confirm your understanding as we talk.

Help them be active listeners. We can ask others to confirm in their own words what they've heard us say. If they have not understood, we should try a fuller explanation that may help them understand both our words and our context.

3. Plan the communication process to minimize mixed messages

If we want to improve our communication process in ways that enhance our ability to solve problems, we will need to think about why we want to communicate in the first place, what we need to learn or transmit, which channels or forums to use, and how we will communicate. We will need to implement our plans and monitor the results.

Clarify our purposes. We frequently convey messages that work at cross purposes when we have interests that genuinely conflict with each other. A professional woman would like to be successful at the office. She might also like to see herself as a full-time nurturing mother, an author, a loving wife, and an outstanding civic leader. As she communicates her honest interests to her family and colleagues, one message may undermine another so that she appears insincere.

Be honest about ambivalence. Even when we intend to build a good working relationship, it is too much to expect that every message we send will be consistent with that goal. Life is too intricate, and human beings too human. Our minds may move on to other things, or we may become defensive and say things we later regret. Whatever our motivation, the result is that we are bound to transmit some mixed messages. Like the old nursery rhyme, we say one thing — and then say something quite to the contrary:

Mother, may I go out to swim?
Yes, my darling daughter.
Hang your clothes on a hickory limb
And don't go near the water.

While we may not be able to avoid inconsistency in our goals, we can reduce the inconsistency in our communication. Here, the best guidance is to clarify our purposes to ourselves, to be honest, and to communicate clearly and carefully. If we don't know whether we would rather go out to dinner with our spouse or stay home with the children, there is no need to tell our spouse one thing and the children another; we can be straightforward with everyone about our mixed feelings. If management is struggling with the tension between cutting costs and preserving jobs, clear and honest statements about the problem will do more for the company's working relationship with its employees than telling everybody what they want to hear.

Convert long-term interests into short-term actions. If apparently urgent situations seem more essential than the important and ongoing task of maintaining a good working relationship with you, I need to build in ways to make the important become more urgent — to put "relationship-building communication" on the agenda. Some cultures, such as the Arab, automatically place relationship-building high on their agenda. A decision to do business with someone is often treated as though it were a decision to form a partnership or get married. In the United States, however, and in many other places, relationship-building (except, perhaps, in the case of courtship) is a long-term objective that regularly loses out to short-term concerns.

The best general advice to make sure that long-term considerations have an impact on what happens today is to develop an immediate operational proposal that responds to the long-term concern. (If it looks as though there will be a shortage of oak firewood in fifty years, let's start planting acorns tomorrow morning at eight.) Similarly, the best advice to make sure that long-term relationship concerns hold their own in the battle of mixed messages is to develop an immediate message that reflects the long-term concerns: To improve the relationship, who should say what to whom? when? and how? I can look at each element of a good working relationship through the lens of communication and ask, for example, what I might say in the immediate future that would improve understanding, reliability, or acceptance. The focus on communication gives us a handle for converting elements like understanding, which may seem vague or abstract, into proposals for immediate decision. Suppose that in a personal relationship I have an insufficient understanding of your goals. To deal with that weakness in an operational way, I can ask myself what I might *communicate* to you today. Perhaps I should invite you to have breakfast with me tomorrow morning at eight o'clock.

Use privacy to minimize the problem of multiple audiences. When we try to talk to many people at the same time, our messages are bound to be confused. When the president of the United States, for example, is making a public statement nominally directed to the Soviet Union, he is aware that his statement will also be heard and noted by, among others:

- the secretaries of state and defense;
- senators and members of Congress;
- those who select stories for the evening television news;
- a large number of American voters; and
- our European allies.

At any one time, the purpose of a given communication may be primarily to have an impact on one or another of those audiences. But when a presidential message to the Soviet Union has been edited and revised in an attempt to satisfy all of them, the final text may end up murky to all. Worse, that text is likely to be accompanied by background statements and television interviews of various other officials, each of whom has a different audience in mind. The resulting "message" is unlikely to improve the president's ability to work with the Soviet Union.

Especially when many audiences are interested in the outcome of a decision, it may be wise to establish a private problem-solving forum to minimize the amount of public discussion during the decision-making process. For example, as part of the arms control agreements between the United States and the Soviet Union, the two superpowers set up the Standing Consultative Commission as a private, closed-door forum for issues of compliance and implementation. While the commission has not worked perfectly, for a period of years it was able to resolve every issue that was brought to it, issues that might otherwise have interfered with the overall superpower relationship. It has been a place for private communication where the United States and the Soviet Union can talk to each other, and *only* each other.

At every level, the confusion that comes from dealing with multiple audiences can be reduced by avoiding the multiple audience and by increasing the amount of one-on-one private discussion. In a family situation, the same principle applies. If you have difficulty working through an issue with your mother-in-law when your spouse is present, consider having a one-on-one lunch. The difference between a talk among three people and a talk between two is enormous. Among three people, every comment is directed to two listeners. There is no chance, for example, to say something to your mother-in-law without the risk that your spouse will react, respond, or change the subject.

Plan encounters to minimize emotional interference. Planning can build confidence and reduce anxiety about communication in general.

Plan an approach to troublesome questions. We can reduce fears of revealing too much or our own uncertainty by thinking things through in advance. For example, suppose I am negotiating to buy a house that I want so desperately that I am willing to pay much more than the market value. I fear that the seller will ask me to name the highest price I would be willing to pay. I may plan an approach to any such question along the following lines:

> I don't want to close my mind on that subject. You may be able to persuade me that your house is worth more than I now think it is. And if you were to pay any attention to some figure I named as the highest I would pay, you would be encouraging me to name a very low figure and try to deceive you. Let me tell you this: I like the house. If I can afford to do so, I will pay what it's worth. Let's discuss what it's worth.

These are not lines I memorize, but having thought through this approach, I no longer fear questions about the most I would pay (or, if I am a seller, the least I would take). Similarly, if I am afraid of divulging sensitive information, I can prepare a safe way to deal with that subject.

Think ahead about candor. If I want to understand you, I will want you to talk about yourself. If I have thought ahead of time about what might be troubling you or why you might be reluctant to talk, I can prepare what I might say to make you more comfortable talking with me. I may want to reveal a bit of personal information about myself and then be open to listening should you want to talk; such as:

My husband and I went through some tough times two years ago, and it affected me so much that I couldn't get myself out of bed in the morning. I stopped exercising, eating well, and visiting friends. But after several months, therapy began to help.

In many situations, such as in dealing with a friend who has just been divorced, I can predict that a large emotional element is likely to affect our communication. The more I think in advance about those emotions, and about what I want to learn and what I want to convey, the better our communication is likely to be and the better able we will be to deal with substantive problems.

Plan where and how to communicate. If we are part of a relationship that is not working well, we may have a pattern of communication that is both ineffective and difficult to break. One way to avoid verbal logjams is to create in advance a forum that will facilitate clear communication.

Such a forum might be on neutral ground to promote a sense of security, equality, and mutual respect, and thus reduce anxiety. A known place and context, which can help people treat otherwise emotional issues in a familiar and businesslike manner, can improve the clarity and quality of communication. It helps to have a regular place, time, and process. Unions and management frequently create committees to deal with workers' grievances. Two companies that work together sometimes designate one person from each to handle jointly any problem that may come up between them. Married couples may designate a particular time of the week to discuss their individual calendars and any issues that may have accumulated. One couple agreed to discuss all divisive issues in the meat department of a nearby supermarket where they had once resolved a major argument. For them, the place had a "spirit of agreement" about it, and each was confident that tempers would stay under control. Anticipating and preparing for divisive issues in some way can alleviate negative patterns that prevent effective communication.

Even if we don't prepare a particular place for sensitive conversations, we may want to set forth some ground rules that will make each of us feel more secure. During a dispute, one person may not want to advance a suggestion for fear that it will be taken as a commitment. In these circumstances, it may help to designate a time and place for brainstorming only — a session in which either person can suggest any solution or wild idea without commitment or attribution.

Implementation: monitor communications with the relationship in mind. As carefully as we might design the communications process to improve the relationship, we may still fall shy of our goal. But we can do better over time if we monitor our communications and take steps to correct problems.

If improving the U.S.-Soviet relationship is in fact a major goal of U.S. foreign policy, for example, some specific person, even a fairly junior official, might be designated the advocate for communication to improve the relationship. The advocate could prepare a plan, generate suggestions to implement it, and monitor the messages and actions of others in the government to make sure they are as consistent as possible with each other and with long-term goals. The advocate could suggest ways to improve the working relationship: What channels of communication should be established? What occasions for two-way discussion should be scheduled? Short-term goals could be discussed in the context of a long-term communication strategy. The United States and the Soviet Union could go further and establish a small joint task force to devise ways in which the two governments could increase the effectiveness of their communication.

Smaller institutions, such as businesses and trade unions, could also benefit from organized thinking about a communication program intended to improve their working relationships. Even in the case of two individuals at the office, it may be useful to do some planning about communication. Such a plan might be a simple checklist along the following lines:

Notes for Improving My Relationship with the New Account Manager

---

COMMUNICATION

1. **Acceptance.** Make sure she knows that she's a member of the team and that I am interested in her point of view.
2. **Frequency.** Speak with her every day.
3. **Audience.** Talk *with* her, not about her. If there is anything I might say to others about her, arrange a time to talk about it with her. Identify goals for the future. Give her constructive feedback about her performance.
4. **Listen.** What's on her mind? Share my perceptions with her and ask how she sees the same things. Does she understand my concerns? Ask her to try to spell them out.
5. **Quality time.** Every now and then, set aside a fair amount of time — perhaps a lunch — for an unhurried discussion of what's on her mind.
6. **Consult.** Before making any decision that might have a significant impact on her, ask for her advice. Repeat it back in my words to make sure she knows I am listening and interested.

Communication is the lifeblood of a working relationship. No matter how good our communication is now, we can undoubtedly find ways to improve it. Common barriers to effective communication — such as assuming there is no need to talk, communicating one-way, and sending mixed messages — can be worn away by planning and active listening. But the simplest and most powerful rule of thumb is to consult the relationship partner. Really consult. Ask advice before making a decision — and listen carefully.

7 | Reliability

Be wholly trustworthy, but not wholly trusting

TRUST IS OFTEN SEEN as the single most important element of a good working relationship. A high level of trust may permit me to accept your statements without question and rely on your promises. Trust among financial institutions and brokers permits them to close thousands of deals every day with a simple handshake or a few words over the telephone. Trust between two governments may allow each to rely on the other for military and economic support, freeing each to pursue economic and social policies that would not otherwise be possible.

At the other extreme, a high level of distrust in a relationship both creates problems and makes them difficult to solve. If I distrust you, I may not want to deal with you at all. I may believe that working out my problems on my own is safer than reaching an agreement with you. How can we negotiate if anything you say may be false? Why try to reach an agreement if I can't trust you to keep it? We all appreciate the value of mutual trust and the cost of mutual suspicion.

Most of our relationships fall somewhere between the extremes of total confidence and deep suspicion. In almost every case, we would welcome a higher level of trust. Yet it is not clear how we can improve trust.

Trust and suspicion are in our heads: they are states of mind. We may sometimes think that in a relationship our goal is trust — to have a wholly trusting state of mind. But that would be dangerous. What we want is not just trust, but well-founded trust. It is not enough to pursue the desired state of mind. We also need to build a foundation for that trust and to balance trust with appropriate skepticism.

Your distrust of me may be caused in part by my conduct, and in part by what goes on in your head independent of my conduct. If I want to increase the level of well-founded trust you have in me, I will want to improve the reliability of my conduct and increase the accuracy of your perception of that conduct. Similarly, my trust in you depends in part on what you actually do and in part on how I assess and think about what you do. A practical goal for a working relationship, and one that each partner can pursue unconditionally, is thus:

1. a high degree of reliability in the behavior of each, and
2. an accurate assessment by each of the risks of relying on the other.

The first part of this chapter considers the question of our own reliability — what may be causing others to distrust us and what we can do about it. The second part considers the question of our partner's reliability — what may be causing our distrust and, again, what we may be able to do about it. A brief third part looks at systems that can either breed distrust or reward reliability.

DEALING WITH OUR OWN RELIABILITY

Our conduct: They may have reason to mistrust us

We almost always think of the problem of trust as being whether the *other* side is trustworthy. In any relationship, there is only one person over whom I have a reasonable amount of control and whose trustworthiness I can definitely improve — me. The behavior I can most easily modify is my own.

Is our conduct erratic? One general meaning of untrustworthy is unpredictable — for whatever reason. Wholly apart from any question of dishonesty or deception, my conduct may in fact be hard to predict because I do different things at different times. It is in this sense that we do not trust the weatherman. We do not doubt his good faith, his diligence in working on his charts, or his honesty in telling us what he thinks is going to happen. We just don't fully believe his predictions. In the same sense, we may not trust brokers who tell us what stocks to buy or what the stock market is going to do. In both cases, they are dealing with phenomena that are difficult to predict.

Human behavior is also difficult to predict. Even my own behavior will sometimes catch me by surprise. The passage of time, new perceptions, and changed circumstances will cause me to say or do things that I, myself, could not have predicted a few weeks earlier. You will be even less able than I to predict my actions, even if you know me well.

Do we communicate carelessly? We can damage our credibility by saying things that others will interpret as commitments when we in fact do not intend to commit ourselves. If you ask me when I am coming home and I reply, "I *should* be home by eleven o'clock," you may interpret that as a commitment and plan to do something with me at eleven-thirty. I may believe that I was giving you only my best estimate, that I had not committed myself. Whether or not your interpretation was reasonable, my communication was sloppy. If I frequently make statements that I do not intend as commitments but that you might reasonably interpret as such, then you have reason to believe that I am unreliable.

Do we treat even clear promises lightly? Where a promise is both intended and clearly understood, there is still a problem because different people give different weight to the importance of keeping a promise. Here, again, the difficulty lies not in deliberate deception, but in being unable to understand how others see things now or how they will see them in the future. Every promise has implicit conditions. You and I promise to have lunch on Tuesday. Each of us will feel some commitment, but we will also feel free to break the date if something sufficiently important (in our eyes) comes up. If you are sick, if the president summons you to Washington, or if any of a large number of unexpected possibilities occurs, you will cancel our commitment.

Suppose I agree to be a surrogate mother. For a fee of $10,000 I agree to bear an infant conceived by artificial insemination for a childless couple. By the time the baby is born, I have changed my mind. I want to keep the baby, finding my emotional obligation to the child I bore greater than the obligation under the contract. Neither I nor anyone else expected this to happen. My "untrustworthiness" stems not from any dishonesty or deception, but from circumstances I did not foresee. Differences arise when we have differing perceptions of just how serious a commitment is and just how important something must be to justify breaking it.

Are we deceptive or dishonest? You may reasonably distrust me if I have intentionally misled you or lied to you. I may have deceived you by telling a lie, making a promise I did not intend to keep, or saying something that was technically correct but intentionally misleading. I may have had good reasons for misleading you. Perhaps I promised someone to keep a secret or did not want to embarrass you. Or I may have lied to cover up some mistake or failure on my part: "I tried to call several times but couldn't get through." "The check is in the mail." "I'm sorry, but I never got the message." "I'm positive I locked the door." Or perhaps I am setting you up to cheat you in the future.

A little bit of dishonesty can create a lot of distrust. If one statement of mine in a hundred is false, you may choose not to rely on me at all. Unless you can develop a theory of when I am honest and when I am not, your discovery of a small dishonesty will cast doubt over everything I say and do.

Improve trustworthiness by improving conduct

It is in my interest to be trusted. If I am worthy of your trust — whether or not you are worthy of mine — my conduct will generate fewer disputes. If I do not deceive you, you will have less reason to get angry with me and deceive me in return. If I am reliable, and you know it, my words will have a greater power to influence you. You will give more weight to my factual statements and more weight to my promises. You will be less suspicious, and we will be better able to deal well with disputes.

The benefits of being reliable even with someone who is not are illustrated by the relationship between a mother and a child. At a young age, a child may be unreliable, prone to say things that are not true, and apt to forget promises. Even so, the more reliable the mother, the greater her ability to influence the child. The child will believe her and take her promises seriously. It would make things easier if the child could also be trusted; but whether or not a child can be trusted, the more trustworthy the mother, the better off she is.

Once I decide to enhance my own trustworthiness in the eyes of someone with whom I wish to have a good working relationship, the task itself is not too difficult. Four rules of thumb are useful to remember: be predictable, be clear, take promises seriously, and be honest.

Be predictable. If our behavior may appear confusing, indecisive, or erratic, we should work to improve our predictability. This may mean setting up a schedule or narrowing the focus of our activities. Even when we cannot predict our own behavior, however, we can follow predictable procedures for making decisions that help our friends understand our actions. The outcome of a criminal trial may be unpredictable, but the process through which the decision is made is very predictable and enhances public confidence in the outcome.

Consultation prior to decision, as outlined more thoroughly in Chapter 6, is a process of informing others that adds predictability to any conduct. Former West German Chancellor Helmut Schmidt described in his memoirs how former President Gerald Ford used consultation to improve his reliability: "Under his Presidency, the United States became, from Bonn's point of view, a more predictable and reliable partner and leader of the Atlantic Alliance. Gerald Ford never surprised me with one-sided decisions taken without consultation" (*New York Times,* December 13, 1987).

Be clear. If we do not intend to make a commitment, we should be careful not to use language that others might reasonably interpret as one. Often, we can affirmatively state that we do not intend to make a commitment. If I do not know when I will finish work, for example, rather than saying, "I *should* be home at eleven o'clock," I can say, "I can't make a commitment. If all goes well, I may be home at eleven, but I may be later." If I am clear about what I mean and what I say, there is less chance that you will find my statements misleading.

Take promises seriously. The more seriously we treat our own commitments the more seriously others will treat them. The easiest way to enhance our reputation for credibility is to make fewer promises. A second and somewhat more difficult step is to be scrupulous about keeping those promises we do make, even when they may seem unimportant. When Robert McNamara was secretary of defense, he made it a point to arrive on time for all meetings. His reputation for reliability on small things that people could see spilled over to enhance his credibility with respect to commitments that were not so easily verifiable.

Be honest. Honesty is indispensable to a good working relationship. Its only cost is the lost possibility of a one-shot, short-term gain that I might obtain by deceit. But practicing deceit is no way to build a working relationship. Deception in one encounter is likely to preclude the kind of relationship that would be able to resolve an unending series of problems quickly and efficiently.

Honesty does not require full disclosure. It does, however, require a clear indication of areas about which full disclosure should not be expected and an explanation of why it is not appropriate. In general, greater disclosure between relationship partners makes it easier for them to solve problems and deal with differences, but nondisclosure is sometimes appropriate. A wife may honestly tell her husband that her conversations with clients are confidential and that even the name of a client must be kept secret.

The mayor of a town will find that a general policy of being open with the citizens will help her gain the trust that will enhance her ability to be effective. Her reputation for integrity will not, however, be injured if she explains that she will not disclose the number of plainclothes detectives the town employs, who they are, or where they are operating. A government will not lose credibility for keeping secret those things that ought to be kept secret, like military codes or plans. The rule of thumb remains, be honest about what you do disclose.

Their assessment of our conduct: Are they wrong about our reliability?

No matter how reliable our conduct may or may not be, others may think it worse than it really is. They may exaggerate the seriousness of a misleading statement or a bit of ambiguous conduct. Partisan bias is likely to make things worse. Suppose I let you borrow my car but ask you to fill it with gas before you return it. You return it on Sunday and, although you spent an hour looking for an open gas station, you could not find one. If you leave me a note, thanking me for the car and saying that you were sorry you couldn't find gas, I may suspect your excuse and your reliability. You, however, may believe you kept your promise as well as you could and not realize that I suspect your reliability. Since you are not aware of my suspicions, you are not likely to reassure me — and my bad impression of you may needlessly affect how we deal with each other in the future.

We are all remarkably understanding and forgiving — of our own conduct. This applies not only to simple failures and mistakes but to deliberate deception, dishonesty, and broken promises. Your distrust of me may be well founded, and I may not be admitting it to myself. I am far more likely to explain my distrust of you by your dishonesty than to explain your distrust of me by mine. Remember that I am trying to make my conduct more reliable to improve your perception of my reliability.

Some people believe that they improve their reputation by never admitting a mistake or making an apology. If I treat my unreliable conduct lightly, I will worsen your perception of my reliability. Suppose, for example, that you are my new landlord and that the rent is due on the first of each month. During each of the first four months, however, I pay the rent a week or more late. If, when you call to discuss my late payments, I respond, "Big deal! I never worry about a couple of weeks," you will probably lower still further your opinion of my reliability. Treating misstatements as insignificant is more likely to damage a reputation than help it.

We can further damage our reputation for reliability by deciding what our commitments mean without discussing them with those who will be affected. Suppose I told my wife that unless I telephoned to the contrary, she could expect me home in time for supper at seven. On Saturday evening I come in at seven forty-five. I may argue that "obviously" the 7:00 P.M. rule applies only to weekdays and not to a Saturday, when I go to a baseball game. In thus defending my record for reliability, I in fact damage it. It would be better for my reputation to acknowledge the possibility of misunderstanding, apologize for any inconvenience my wife suffered, and clarify the practice for the future.

Help them perceive our conduct as trustworthy

We can help our relationship partners trust us by the honesty with which we talk about our conduct, and we can enhance our reputation by openly discussing conduct that might look to others as inconsistent with a prior promise. A supplier, for example, can strengthen his credibility by dealing with what might be thought of as late deliveries:

> We said we would deliver that summer furniture before Memorial Day. It occurred to me that you might be expecting delivery by Saturday, May 23, since Memorial Day is being observed this year on Monday the 25th rather than on May 30, the traditional day. Delivering the furniture by May 23 would be extremely difficult for me, but I can do it by the 27th. I wanted you to know, and I do hope it will be all right.

It is particularly valuable, as in the above example, to deal honestly with problems *before* they happen. If it is going to be difficult for me to meet a commitment, my conduct will look better if I let you know about the problem as soon as possible. I build your confidence in my reliability by letting you know that there is a problem, that you don't have to worry about it, and that I'm doing something about the situation. If I am falling behind on some matter and dreading a client's call, I should take the initiative and call the client, tell her that I have not yet been able to get to that matter, and give her a new estimate of when I will deal with it.

I can do a great deal to make myself more trustworthy, both in fact and in your eyes. To be more reliable and to build your perception of my reliability are both unconditionally constructive. Such conduct is good for the working relationship and good for me whether or not you do anything to make yourself more worthy of my trust.

On the other hand, I would like you, too, to be worthy of trust. Why may I find you untrustworthy, and what might I do about that?

DEALING WITH THEIR RELIABILITY

Their conduct: Do we encourage their unreliable conduct?

Right off the bat we need to recognize that we can do less about making the other side reliable than we can do about ourselves. But our perception that they are untrustworthy may be a major impediment to a working relationship, and it would be a mistake to throw up our hands in despair. We may be able to affect the actual conduct of others for the better, and we can certainly do a great deal about how we think about the risks of trusting them and what we do about those risks.

Just as my behavior may justify, at least in part, your assessment of my reliability, so your behavior may justify my view that you are unreliable. And it is possible that I may be behaving in ways that cause you to be less reliable than you would otherwise be.

Do we overload trust? Sometimes we trust others when it is counterproductive to do so. Leaving money around an office increases the temptation for others to pick it up. Businesses long ago learned the value of auditors. The U.S. Customs Service knows that many people entering the country would be less trustworthy if they were trusted too much — if they knew that there would be no customs inspection. State police know that even law-abiding Americans would be more likely to exceed the speed limit if there were no patrol cars.

In family relations, wise parents know that raising children with no rules and little supervision — trusting young children to establish and monitor their own guidelines — overloads trust and increases the likelihood that the child will become less and less worthy of that trust. The same is true in business and other relationships.

In the negotiation of international arms control agreements, there has been widespread recognition of the danger of overloading trust, leading to an emphasis on verification of compliance. The fear of overloading trust has sometimes been so great that it has precluded *any* agreements, even when the terms would clearly serve the interests of each superpower.* While this position is extreme, the basic concern is sound: we can aggravate the problem of mistrust by trusting more than we should.

Do we trust too little? Most of us recognize the danger of trusting too much. But we often underestimate the danger of trusting too little. A parent who helps a child do everything perfectly, or tries to protect a child from any risk, decreases the child's responsibility and diminishes the likelihood that the child will become worthy of trust. Why should the child look both ways before crossing a street if someone else always does it? The same is true of an employer who supervises an employee too closely. In some factories, the addition of quality control inspectors has caused production workers to pay *less* attention to quality because "it's not my job."

---

*Some people assume that no agreed restraints are worthwhile unless there is 100 percent verification and that such verification is not only necessary but sufficient to assure compliance. The truth is far more complex. In some cases, perfect verification may neither be necessary nor sufficient. In the case of the proposed comprehensive ban on nuclear testing, for example, all recognize that perfect verification is impossible. It would be possible for either side to place a small nuclear device in an underground cavern and wait for the test to be triggered by a large earthquake, which would conceal the explosion. But the risks to international security from such an undetected test may be far less than those resulting from unrestricted underground testing of nuclear weapons. If so, a comprehensive test ban might be a good idea even if full verification is impossible. But even if full verification were possible, it might not be enough to assure compliance. A country that wanted to test might well do so despite the political cost of having it known that it broke its promise.

We damage someone's trustworthiness by not trusting at all. It is risky *not* to take risks. How much to trust others is a separate question, discussed below, but it is important to recognize that we can affect conduct by trusting either too much or too little.

Do we criticize no matter what they do? Routine attacks on a relationship partner for unreliability are common, and they usually reflect a double standard. We forgive ourselves and our friends, but judge harshly the conduct of others.

Such routine criticism often represents the honest expression of partisan perceptions. But if I hope to develop a better working relationship with my adversaries, criticizing them as unreliable is not likely to make them more reliable. Broad statements of distrust ("We can't trust the Russians") are likely to reduce rather than increase their incentive to be honest and reliable. If the Soviets are going to be so charged no matter what they do, they may think, "Why should we go out of our way to comply with some technical provision of an agreement when the United States will charge us with noncompliance anyway?"

Attacking the trustworthiness of others — judging their conduct as worse than it really is — damages the potential for a working relationship in several ways. First, as noted above, unjustified accusations of unreliability reduce any incentive to be reliable. (In contrast, private discussions of a genuine concern, in which there is open listening as well as talking, are likely to be constructive.) Second, public charges of untrustworthiness are likely to generate anger and lead to countercharges. In a mud-slinging contest, no one comes out with a clean reputation.

Finally, excessive charges of untrustworthiness lower the community standard. Even a mistaken belief that "everybody is doing it" soon becomes self-fulfilling. As rumors circled Wall Street in the 1980s that some brokerage firms were engaged in insider trading, others found it easier to do the same. As rumors built, more people became dishonest. Even the most prestigious brokerage houses became involved in illegal practices.

Help them be more reliable

Despite serious limits on how much we can do to improve the honesty and reliability of others, some things are possible.

Do not overload trust; act to reduce risks. It is pleasant to be able to trust someone, but it is a great mistake to be too trusting. The greater the reliance on "pure trust," the greater the chance that it will be misplaced — that it will break under the weight. Whatever a homeowner's credit record, a bank, before lending a significant sum, is likely to ask for a mortgage on the house. The wise landlord will ask a tenant for a security deposit. Such security arrangements limit the damage if a promise is broken. Often more important, they reduce the likelihood that it will be.

Trust them when they deserve it. If I am not trusting you enough, the problem is likely to be my aversion to risk rather than your lack of trustworthiness. No matter how skillfully you drive a car, I may feel safer when I am driving. No matter how carefully you lock the back door, I may want to check it. If I am averse to risk, I am likely to err on the side of trusting you too little.

If, for whatever reason, I trust you less than you deserve, you are likely to become less trustworthy, resentful, or both, and I will have damaged our ability to work together. To minimize this damage, I will want to explain to you my view of the risks, listen to yours, and find ways to satisfy my concerns while still showing you the trust and confidence you deserve. My goal is to enhance the reliability of your *behavior* by granting you as much trust as I can reasonably justify and letting you know that I am doing so.

Give both praise and blame — precisely. To the extent that our words can affect the behavior of others, that effect will be greater when praise and blame are handed out appropriately and with precision. People are more likely to behave reliably if they know that their reliability is appreciated. The satisfaction of getting affirmative recognition for reliable conduct will often exceed any satisfaction that might come from ignoring a commitment.

For criticism — positive or negative — to be effective, it should be fair, accurate, and directed to specific behavior. If the only positive feedback you ever hear from me is, "Job well done," you may question if I am sincere or whether I have some automatic policy or ulterior motive for praising you. If, however, the feedback is illustrated ("You did a great job on that quarterly report. Your analysis of our changing product mix was so clearly and concisely written that it will help us in our long-range planning"), you will understand both the basis of my opinion and the behavior I would like you to repeat (or avoid) in the future.

If we give fair, accurate, and illustrated positive feedback, then any negative feedback (equally fair and clear) is more likely to be effective. If all you ever hear is negative criticism, you may assume that I am just a negative person or that I have it in for you, and that your behavior has little to do with my words. Or you may assume that I am criticizing you for political purposes. Whatever your explanation, you are likely to ignore criticism that is consistently negative.

Treat problematic conduct as a joint problem, not a crime. Criticism looks back at past conduct and leads to recriminations. We will do more to improve an ongoing relationship if we treat every broken promise as a matter of future concern — as an ongoing question for the relationship. It is never too late to affect the future. We are more likely to do so to the extent that we:

- look forward, not back;
- are specific, not general; and
- talk about conduct, not people.

If you show up an hour late for a dinner date, I could judge your conduct, generalize from it, and draw conclusions about your character: "Late again! No wonder nobody trusts you." An alternative is to explain my concerns and perceptions in a reasonable tone and to seek your advice about how we should deal with time commitments in the future:

> I have been waiting almost an hour. Did something come up? It would help me plan my time and avoid my getting upset if we could be clear about our time commitments. Perhaps I was unclear in my invitation. Would it be better if I tried to reconfirm time and place? Or perhaps you could call me if you are going to be late. What would you suggest?

Each incident of apparent unreliability provides an opportunity to work together, both on "picking up the pieces" of this event and structuring ways to reduce the likelihood of such occurrences in the future.

Our assessment of their conduct: Do we evaluate it wrongly?

How much we trust those on the other side of our relationship depends not only on their actual conduct but on what goes on in our heads. No matter how reliable your actual conduct may be, the way I think about it may aggravate the problem of distrust.

Do we misperceive their behavior? More often than not, we underestimate another person's trustworthiness. Patients don't trust doctors, voters don't trust politicians, and almost nobody trusts lawyers. It takes very little to create suspicion and a lot to put it to rest. In negotiation training exercises, a group of colleagues — fellow executives, union members, students, or others — is divided into teams and put in different rooms, and almost immediately each team begins to suspect the worst of the other. Whatever the basis for suspicion, the amount typically exceeds that which is justified by the other's behavior.

Nevertheless, people are sometimes too trusting. Some of us are likely to judge a friend's reliability by his open smile, his pleasant manner, or the length of the relationship. Confidence men make a living off the gullible. Politicians and police are sometimes trusted beyond the level warranted by either their integrity or their competence. Banks, stores, and businesses lose large sums of money every year through embezzlement by trusted employees.

While distrust impedes the ability of two people to deal well with their differences, the problem cannot be solved by trusting someone who does not deserve it.

Do we confuse different kinds of unpredictability? The concept of distrust is sufficiently general that we may confuse one kind with another. If conduct is unpredictable, we may think the person is untrustworthy. If a person is untrustworthy, we begin to question his honesty. Once we have thought in terms of honesty, that concern spreads to other areas. We dump all "trust" issues into one pot — and it spills over into situations that are remarkably different. A company that has been (perhaps unavoidably) late in shipping its products finds that customers begin to suspect the quality of the products themselves and sometimes the integrity of the company's personnel. Distrust is infectious.

It is useful to distinguish among different grounds for concern.

Incompatible intentions. If I say that I do not trust Harry, it may simply mean that Harry and I are competing for the same job and I cannot assume that his intentions toward me are benevolent. When an American business executive says that he cannot trust the Japanese, he is likely to mean that he fears that a Japanese company will succeed in taking markets away from his own company.

Forgetfulness. Children as a class are likely to be less trustworthy than adults: they may treat commitments less seriously or simply forget them if their attention is elsewhere. Among adults, it is not only absent-minded professors who are untrustworthy in this sense. Memories fail. When we are busy working on one subject, we often forget appointments, bills, and other mundane obligations.

Unpredictability. Some people run their lives according to well-developed habits and carefully planned schedules. Others are more spontaneous and variable. We often think of the first type of person as being more reliable than the second type, even though the latter may in fact pay equal or greater attention to commitments than the former.

Do we judge morality rather than risk? In deciding whether to trust someone — whether, for example, to lend him money — we often focus on that person's moral qualities. Is he a good person? That question is highly relevant but should rarely be decisive. Good people can go bankrupt. If my dearest friend is unable to repay a loan, I may be unable to afford the loss. And a note secured by a mortgage may be a sound investment, even though I know little or nothing about the moral goodness of the borrower. The decision to trust a borrower, or a child or an ally, should be based on an analysis of the benefits and risks involved. Moral integrity is likely to be a critical ingredient in selecting those with whom I want to have a relationship and in assessing risks, but it is well to remember that it may be neither a necessary nor a sufficient basis for trust.

Base trust on risk analysis, not moral judgment

Gain an accurate perception of their conduct. No matter how reliable or unreliable the other side may be, we will be able to deal with our differences better if we can predict their behavior. Either too much or too little confidence in their reliability will interfere with joint problem-solving. To make an accurate prediction, we need to look realistically at their interests, their words and promises, and their past patterns of conduct — as free of our partisan perceptions as possible. What follows is not a comprehensive system for assessing reliability but a few guidelines.

Distinguish among kinds of unreliability. As suggested earlier, people can be unreliable in different ways. They can be erratic, ambiguous, secretive, misleading, deceptive, or dishonest, or they may weigh promises lightly in the face of changed circumstances. The way in which others are unreliable — whether like children or like confidence men — should make a crucial difference in how we deal with them.

In addition to the distinctions made earlier, two points are important:

Distinguish hostile intentions from dishonesty. Your wishing me ill rather than well need not interfere with our working relationship. We would like to be able to deal well even with those with whom we have fundamental disagreements. Even hostile intentions can be reliable.

The U.S. government might like to see the Communist government in China replaced with a non-Communist one. Presumably the Chinese government would like to see a government in Washington that accepted a socialist ideology. Those incompatible objectives need not interfere with the ability of the two governments to deal honestly with those differences and with others, such as those over trade, immigration, and international terrorism.

In the business world, Chrysler might well like to drive Ford out of business, just as a corner grocery store might well wish ill for a nearby supermarket. Two executives, aspiring for the same job, might well have intentions that conflict, just as might two young men courting the same woman. In every case, there is ground for "distrusting" the other's intentions. But aims that conflict need not stand in the way of the kind of reliability that will help solve mutual problems. Incompatible objectives, like incompatible values and perceptions, generate conflicts that we should be able to handle. We do not need others to wish us well (as pleasant as that might be). What we need is honesty.

In trying to build a working relationship, conflicting intentions are less of a problem than deception about them. If someone is pretending to be my friend and supporter when I have grounds for believing that she wishes me ill and is acting contrary to my interests, I properly distrust her. If she falsely denies that any conflicts exist, we will not deal well with our differences. If, however, she is open about her goals and I have a well-founded basis for believing in her honesty — that she believes what she says and that when she makes a promise she intends to carry it out — we can solve problems jointly. Serious conflicting interests should not stand in the way of advancing shared ones, as when labor and management try to avoid bankruptcy, or when the Soviet Union and the United States try to avoid nuclear war. It will help reduce mistrust if we distinguish between hostile intentions and deception.

Distinguish unpredictability from dishonesty. If we are to build the kind of trust needed for a good working relationship, we must maintain the distinction between predictability and honesty. It is possible for me to be perfectly honest and highly unpredictable. I may be quixotic, forgetful, make few promises, and treat those I make far less seriously than you would like. The reverse is also true: it is possible for people to be dishonest, yet quite predictable. For more than a year, a father needed no alarm clock. He could rely on his three-year-old daughter to wake him up before seven every morning no matter what she said the night before. She may have threatened to let him oversleep and miss his plane or she may have promised to let him sleep late because it was Sunday. It made no difference. She would wake him up between six and seven. The father could not trust her at the age of three but, in this respect, he could rely on her completely.

If unforeseen circumstances have caused you to break a promise, I should not conclude that you are a dishonest person. If you meant what you said when you said it, you spoke honestly. Suppose I, a young doctor, accept a particular position "trusting" that a senior doctor will give me excellent training and will continue to generate a large research budget. He has told me, honestly, that he plans to stay around for years. Yet if on short notice he accepts an important new job in Washington, leaving me in the lurch, I should distinguish clearly between his change of plans and any issue of dishonesty, deception, or untrustworthiness. I may have relied on the assumption that he would continue to work with me, but his shift of position did not reveal any moral fault. His change of plans may discomfit me, but he no more deserves an adverse moral judgment than the meteorologist whose failure to forecast a shower ruined my picnic. We should think clearly about the reasons for disappointments and avoid a general mistrust that can spread contagiously and unfairly to other areas.

At the international level, it is equally important not to confuse the degree of unpredictability with the different factors that may be causing it. For years, both the Soviet Union and the United States found each other's conduct difficult to predict. Americans found many Soviet actions difficult to predict because of the high degree of secrecy in Soviet decision-making. Soviets found U.S. action equally difficult to predict because of the rapid turnover in government officials and the American penchant for tackling problems afresh in ways that give little weight to prior statements of policy. Each side would be wrong to confuse the other's unpredictability with dishonesty.

Rely on risk analysis. Determining how much I should trust you is a question of assessing risk, not morality. Doubts about your honesty and commitment will affect my analysis of the risks involved in extending trust. And since I can probably rely on you to act in your own self-interest, I will consider carefully the interests at stake as I think you will weigh them. Deciding whether or not to make a particular decision that involves my "trusting" some statement or promise of yours is primarily a task of weighing the risks and the competing costs and benefits.

Some risks are well worth taking wholly independent of the integrity of the people involved. It is better to get into the lifeboat with someone about whom I have doubts than to go down with the ship. Other risks, however, should not be undertaken even when dealing with the most honorable and upright people. I may have perfect confidence in the moral integrity of a good friend, but if he knows little about airplanes, I should not trust him to fly me home. And if he doesn't know how to run a business, I should not invest my life savings in his new company.

Leaving aside all questions of affection or dislike, I should assess the risks of reliance against the risks of not relying. How large is the potential downside loss or damage on each side of the choice? And what are the potential benefits? Treating reliance as a matter of risk analysis rather than moral judgment is a good course for decisions at every level, from personal to governmental.

DEALING WITH SYSTEMS
THAT AFFECT RELIABILITY

Systems sometimes discourage reliability

In some instances, the mistrust that may pervade a relationship stems not from the behavior of one party or the perception of another, but from the nature of the incentives imposed on behavior by a social or economic system. For example, my company may buy electricity from a utility company. A system of regulation that allows the utility, as a public monopoly, to set its rates at a certain percentage above its costs encourages it to increase costs and to calculate them at the highest possible level. I cannot rely on it to look after my interests. Establishing a different system — competition — would change those incentives radically. The distrust I may feel toward the utility comes from a recognition that the incentives pull in directions that make the system — from my point of view — unreliable.

Strengthen systems that reward reliability

We often fail to appreciate how much a reliable system can serve to overcome a lack of confidence we may have in given individuals or entities. The credit card system enables businesses around the world to rely on millions of individuals who are personally unknown to them. As I drive along a two-lane highway at fifty-five miles an hour, other cars, a few feet away from me, are driving in the opposite direction at an equal or greater speed. I rely on them to stay on their side of the road. Even though I do not know these other drivers or know anything about their reputation and skill, I "trust" them with my life.

When flying across the Atlantic, I trust Soviet pilots and the pilots of all other aircraft over the ocean to respect the rules about altitudes, space between aircraft, and so forth. We have designed a system that makes it in everyone's interest to respect the system. This kind of reliability holds great promise — in personal, business, and international relations.

It may be easier to trust a process than a person. I may trust my brother to be honest and to keep his word, but I know from experience that differences will nonetheless arise. It helps to know that if we disagree and cannot resolve it quickly, the presumption is that we will flip a coin and let that decide the matter. American citizens tend to trust their government to decide a great many questions. But we trust the government even more than we otherwise might because we know that in most cases, if a matter cannot be settled, we can go to the polls or go to court. We have a system for resolving disputes even with the government. We rely more on the system for dealing with our differences than we rely on a promise of the government. And even if we lose, we feel better losing an election or losing in court than losing to the dictate of some government official.

Each of us can do something to improve our own reliability and reduce the role of distrust in any relationship.

Our own conduct should be trustworthy. We can work to be honest and demonstrably reliable. That way we maximize the chance that in each relationship we will be trusted and deserving of trust.

With respect to others, the advice is more complex. We will want to know as much as we reasonably can about the people we are dealing with. If they have been trustworthy in the past, we can more readily assume that they will not intentionally deceive us in the future. But risks remain — risks of misunderstanding, changed circumstances, and unpredictable events. We should be neither more nor less trusting than is justified by the risks. We should go beyond moral assessment and make a careful analysis of the costs and benefits, the risks, and the alternatives. In doing so, we will maximize the chance of balancing healthy skepticism with well-founded trust.

8 | Persuasion, Not Coercion

Negotiate side by side

A dispute once arose between the wind and the sun over which was the stronger of the two. To settle the argument, the sun challenged the wind to a contest: whichever could make a passing traveler take off his coat would be the stronger. The sun was confident of success and let the wind have the first chance.

The sun hid behind a cloud, and the wind blew an icy blast. But the harder the wind blew, the more closely did the traveler wrap his coat around him. At last the wind gave up. Then the sun came from behind the cloud and began to shine down upon the traveler with all its might. The traveler felt the sun's genial warmth, and as he grew warmer and warmer he took off his coat and sat down to rest in the shade.

— "The Wind and the Sun," *Aesop's Fables*

JUST AS MY ABILITY to negotiate with someone is affected by the quality of our relationship, so the quality of the relationship is affected by the way I negotiate. How we try to influence each other has a significant impact on the ability of the relationship to deal with future differences.

132

The way people negotiate can wreck a relationship

One bad negotiation can damage a working relationship for a long time. It is easy to have a good relationship with someone with whom we have no differences. If you and I think alike and have similar interests and values, all will go well — until some issue arises that divides us. At that point we may quarrel. I may let you know that we are going to do it my way "or else." Or I may tell you that one of us is going to have to back down and that it is not going to be me. In an instant I can say or do things that are highly destructive to the relationship. I may win a point in a way that undercuts whatever understanding, effective communication, and mutual trust we may have built up.

Each of us occasionally engages in an exchange with someone over some issue in a way that makes future problem-solving more difficult. We feel frustrated, angry, unhappy with the process, unhappy with the outcome, unhappy with each other, and frequently unhappy with ourselves as well.

To avoid sacrificing a relationship for a short-term gain, we want to use negotiating techniques that protect our interests and, at the same time, are consistent with building a good working relationship. A comprehensive exposition of such techniques is beyond the scope of this book. (Some basic guidelines are contained in another book, *Getting to YES*.) This chapter will focus more narrowly on the negotiation tactics most dangerous to a working relationship — those involving coercion — and alternatives to them.

Coercion tends to damage a working relationship. Chapter 2 identifies six elements in a relationship that tend to enhance problem-solving, of which one is using noncoercive modes of influence. Coercion tends to damage each of the other five elements. To the extent that I feel coerced:

- emotions of anger and frustration become more likely to overwhelm reason;
- mutual understanding becomes less likely;
- there is less need and less chance for effective communication;
- I will find you less trustworthy; and
- I will feel that my interests and views have been rejected.

Coercion tends to damage the quality of an agreement. Often, attempted coercion will preclude agreement. If you try to push me around, I may push back. If you threaten me, I may threaten you. In the history of labor strikes, violent confrontations, and military actions, there are many that testify to the failure of coercion to produce an agreement of any kind.

If I am coerced into accepting an agreement, it is unlikely that that agreement will:

- have been crafted to meet my interests as well as it might have been;
- have had the benefit of any of my creative thinking;
- be legitimate as measured by standards of fairness that appeal to me.

And, in contrast to an agreement that I have been persuaded to accept, a coerced outcome is likely to be less easy to implement and more likely to break down.

A case study may illustrate the problem. Spinthrift Mills, Inc., operates a large textile plant that manufactures shirting fabric. In 1984, Spinthrift suffered a long strike by its largest union, the International Brotherhood of Textile Workers. As part of the strike settlement, Spinthrift agreed to start a profit-sharing plan and to increase worker participation in factory management in exchange for wage concessions.

In 1986, the company was still losing money, largely because of Korean and Chinese competition. Spinthrift's president, George Wade, and its Board of Directors decided that the only way to compete was to invest in new looms, which would reduce labor costs and increase line speeds. Wade ordered the looms for delivery in six months.

Let's look at the "negotiation" that took place three months later. At a quarterly management-labor review meeting, Wade told the union president, Bob Dunlap, about the new looms:

WADE: I want to tell you that the company is spending $15 million on new looms for the shirting lines. We will have to reallocate many of the workers. There will be some layoffs, at least for the short term, but we are hoping that with lower costs we will be able to gain market share and increase production.

DUNLAP: You can no longer make decisions like that without consulting us.

WADE: Look, Bob, there is nothing else we could do to stay competitive. We have already ordered the looms. The decision has been made. We can't back out now.

DUNLAP: You can't do that to us. On behalf of the union I demand that you cancel the order. You are not going to win this one.

WADE: Sooner or later, I have to exercise my judgment as president about what is best for the company. I don't want people to lose their jobs any more than you do, but we have no choice if we want to compete with the Koreans.

DUNLAP: You don't care about people. You drive around in your Cadillac and never see the workers. You've made money off these people for fifty years. Now you've lied to us again. You never meant to give us any voice in the company.

WADE: I know you want to look like a tough union president, but don't get too big for your britches. This issue is nonnegotiable. There is no point in talking about it anymore. If you want to work at this company, you've got to help it survive. You don't have any choice. You know you can't strike. There are hundreds of unemployed workers in this town who would love to take your jobs.

DUNLAP: The minute you put those machines in here, you've got a problem. We may not strike, but we can sure as hell keep those machines from working.

WADE: If one of those machines is damaged, you're fired.

No one would consider this a model negotiation, but what precisely is wrong with it?

Negotiators often use coercive tactics

Just as there is a fundamental difference between dueling and problem-solving, there is a fundamental difference between treating a negotiation as a contest between enemies and treating it as a shared and difficult task for colleagues. Granted: there are conflicting interests, an agreement will require people to change their minds, and emotions may run high. Still, there remains a crucial distinction between trying to bring about a decision by coercion, which operates against the will of another person, and by honest persuasion, which convinces the mind. The line between the two is not sharp and clear; the difference is often one of degree. Yet coercion, however light or strong, tends to damage both the substantive outcome of a negotiation and the ongoing relationship.

The negotiation between Wade and Dunlap illustrates some common coercive tactics.

What was said	Coercive tactic
"You don't care. . . ." ". . . you've lied again." ". . . you want to look . . . tough. . . ." ". . . don't get too big for your britches."	Attack people on the other side.
"You are not going to win. . . ."	Treat negotiation as a contest.
"We can't back out now." "We have already ordered the looms."	Commit early in the negotiation.
". . . I demand. . . ."	Take a position.
". . . we have no choice. . . ." "You don't have any choice." "This issue is nonnegotiable."	Narrow the options to "either/or."
"You know you can't strike." ". . . unemployed workers . . . would love to take your jobs."	Try to break the will of the other side.
". . . we can . . . keep those machines from working." "If one of those machines is damaged, you're fired."	Threaten; worsen their walk-away alternative.

Each of these tactics is coercive. Each attempts to gain a concession, not by jointly addressing the problem, but by unilaterally attacking the person, attempting to break his will, or presenting him with a fait accompli.

No one likes to be coerced. But we still try to coerce others, especially when there is little time or opportunity for persuasion. We may coerce our children by withholding dessert until they finish their supper. We may coerce other drivers at an intersection by pulling out first. We may coerce management by threatening to quit unless we get a higher salary.

Threats are easy to make. Often, they seem to work with little cost. If the other side yields, we get what we want without having to do anything more. If the other side refuses, we can then decide what to do next. Such thinking lures us into using coercive tactics of one form or another despite their frequent failure to produce agreement and despite the predictable negative consequences for the relationship. We use coercive tactics simply because we can't think of any better tactics.

For each of the coercive tactics identified above, there is an alternative approach:

Coercive tactic	Alternative approach
Attack people on the other side.	Attack the problem.
Treat negotiation as a contest.	Treat negotiation as joint problem-solving.
Commit early in the negotiation.	Remain open to persuasion.
Take a position.	Explore interests.
Narrow the options to "either/or."	Invent multiple options.
Try to break the will of the other side.	Try to persuade them of what's fair.
Threaten; worsen their walk-away alternative.	Improve our walk-away alternative.

The rest of this chapter takes a closer look at each of these coercive tactics and the recommended alternative approaches.

Attacking the individual vs. Attacking the problem

Attacking an individual is psychological coercion. A standard negotiating ploy is to direct ad hominem criticism at the person with whom I am negotiating. I may believe that by focusing my attention on you rather than on our substantive differences, I will coerce you into giving in. I try to play on your fear or insecurity: "You obviously don't know what you are doing. I wouldn't want to be in your shoes when your boss hears about this."

It is often easy indeed to attack your actions, your judgment, your honesty, and your character in general. I may even do so without fully realizing it. A clue is when I find myself using "you" frequently, telling you what you really think, what you really want, and what your secret motives may be. Personal attacks are designed to bring psychological pressure on the will of the negotiating partner. All such tactics will feel coercive and tend to damage the ability of the people to work together in the future.

Attack the problem. In every negotiation there are two sets of issues: "people" issues of the kind to which this book is directed (such as rationality, understanding, communication, honesty, and acceptance), and substantive issues involved in the negotiation (such as price, terms, specifications, dates, numbers, and conditions). As Chapter 2 explains, it helps to disentangle these two sets of issues — to separate the people from the problem — and deal separately with each. Too often negotiators are hard on the people and somewhat fuzzy on the problem. Sound advice is to be soft on the people and hard on the problem. In this way, difficulties with the problem need not cause difficulties in the relationship.

One way to make it easier for me to attack a problem without attacking you is for us to sit more or less side by side facing a flip chart, a map, a list of issues, a draft, or some other physical representation of the substantive problem. In this setting, I can jot down points, figures, or arguments and disagree with them forcefully, without criticizing you in any way that is likely to be taken personally and to damage our working relationship.

Winning a contest vs. Solving a problem

Assuming negotiation is a contest leads us to coercion. Many negotiators proceed on the implicit assumption that they are engaged in a contest, like a professional football game, in which someone is going to win and someone is going to lose. If negotiation is taken as a battle, coercive tactics seem appropriate.

Treat negotiation as joint problem-solving. To the extent that two negotiators see themselves as colleagues (with somewhat differing interests) trying to work out a good solution to a difficult problem, they are unlikely to engage in coercive tactics that would damage their relationship. A problem-solving lawyer, seeking to settle litigation between two companies, might start a negotiation with an approach along the following lines:

> Boy, our clients have gotten themselves in a real mess. While our chief litigator is going full steam ahead and is looking for a big victory, my client has asked me to sit down with you and see if we can come up with some kind of settlement that the two of us would recommend to our respective clients. I have no authority to commit my client, and I do not expect you to commit yours.
>
> Do you think we could invent something we would both support?

With that tone, coercive tactics by either side seem inappropriate.

Commit early vs. Remain open

Early commitment says the other must change. A widely used but poor approach in negotiation is for each side, unilaterally and before discussions begin, to lock itself into a particular solution, insisting that agreement is possible only if the other side is flexible: "The decision has been made." "The lowest price I will accept for that car is $3500." "The union will not accept anything less than a 12 percent pay increase." "The president has decided that he will accept no limitation of any kind on his Strategic Defense Initiative."

Some commitments are not coercive, such as one that communicates a firm offer — a statement of what one is willing to do: "I am willing to sell the car for $3500." "The union is willing to accept a 12 percent pay increase." But stating a position does coerce to the extent that it communicates what one is *not* willing to do: "I will not change; if we are going to reach agreement *you* must change." We communicate the same message when we say, "Take it or leave it" or "Do it my way or I won't do it."

The tactic of early commitment is based on the assumption that you would rather have a deal on my terms than no deal. To convince you to accept my terms, all I have to do is to demonstrate sufficient commitment to my position to convince you that I will not change. Perhaps the most common technique for tying my hands is making a public statement: "I will never increase taxes." Other techniques include taking irreversible action. "We have already ordered the looms."

Early commitment sometimes "works." If I give you a take-it-or-leave-it choice, you may take it — this time. But such a tactic is almost certain to be bad for the future. If I routinely commit early to a fixed position and insist that you accept it, you will become increasingly resentful at being pushed around and may respond with a similar tactic. And besides threatening the relationship, an early commitment makes it difficult for me to work out a better agreement later, after I have a better understanding of your interests and we have jointly explored options I had not previously known.

Remain open to persuasion. As noted above, a commitment that conveys what I am *willing* to do may help by opening the negotiation to possible solutions. This will be true only if I am sure to communicate that my offer is not the *only* one I am prepared to accept — I am open to persuasion. If I am about to go into a negotiation, it is useful for me to think through what kind of an agreement I would like to achieve, what terms would be favorable to me that might be acceptable to you, and the standards of fairness that I might advocate and that you might find persuasive. If I know the subject matter well, I might make an early positive commitment to an offer that I am prepared to make. At the same time, I can communicate clearly that I am open to persuasion:

> I am prepared to pay what the house is worth if I can afford it. Judging by recent sales in the neighborhood, the appraisal of a bank, the tax assessment, and an estimate of rental value, I now believe your house is worth between $165,000 and $180,000. Here are my figures and where they came from. Based on that information, I am prepared to make you a firm offer right now, subject only to a termite inspection, to buy your house for $172,500. In addition, if you have objective evidence that suggests the house is worth more than that, I am prepared to consider it.

Such an offer clearly states what I am willing to do and why I think it is fair. It does not, however, lock me into one fixed position or indicate that the only chance for an agreement is for the owner to accept my terms. By negotiating in this way, I can be both firm and open. If the seller feels any coercion, it will be from the objective facts of what the house is worth, not from me.

Focus on positions vs. Explore interests

Positions take the discussion away from interests. If I begin a negotiation by setting out a position, I direct our discussion toward one particular answer rather than first trying to understand the problem. My position is unlikely to take your interests into account. Even if my position remains somewhat flexible, you have not been heard and to that extent may feel coerced.

Many companies and unions open a negotiation by setting out their positions. Yet the practice promotes haggling: positions beget counterpositions. Even the phrase "collective bargaining" suggests that there must be a quid pro quo. Each decision requires bargaining. Neither side will do what it ought to do unless it gets something in exchange. Any family whose members would do what made sense for the family only if they got something in return would find joint problem-solving difficult.

Positional tactics tend to produce outcomes in which both parties compromise their original positions in ways that do not well satisfy their underlying interests. When our interests are left unmet, we often feel as though we "lost" — and the tactics that caused our loss feel coercive. Although in any one situation the coercive effect of focusing on positions may be slight, the cumulative effect of a series of such transactions may seriously undermine a working relationship.

Explore interests. We are more likely to engage in a negotiating process that meets our mutual interests if we discuss those interests. Rather than beginning with some unilaterally determined answers — from which I know you will ask me to back down — we should start off, perhaps in a "prenegotiation" session, with a joint exploration of the various interests involved. What are the different subjects that might be included in an agreement? What are the concerns of the negotiators with respect to each subject?

In this process, the negotiators often find interests that are different but not in conflict with each other, and such differences can lead to solutions. One company may want assets off its books for tax reasons, whereas another may need to boost its assets for regulatory reasons. Joint exploration is more likely to discover such complementary interests than an exchange of gross positions. Exploring interests can also help generate a problem-solving attitude.

Either/or vs. Multiple options

As I limit choices, you feel coerced. Even if I don't commit to a fixed position at the beginning of a negotiation, I may view the process as one in which I should progressively narrow your choices and limit discussion to fewer and fewer options, finally saying that you must choose between two. When I present you with limited options and refuse to consider more, I constrain your freedom, and you will resent it.

Lawyers frequently try to simplify a problem by reducing it to a legal question or by treating a complex situation as "simply a matter of money." The more I tell you that your choices are limited, the more coerced you are likely to feel.

Invent multiple options. The chance that a negotiation will produce a good substantive agreement improves if the negotiators, without commitment, generate a large number of relevant ideas and suggestions. The more options considered, the greater the chance that the parties will find one that well reconciles their differences.

Not only are the substantive results likely to be better, the process will feel less coercive. Both consequences aid the relationship.

Break their will vs. Persuade of what's fair

Trying to break another's will is inherently coercive. In many types of bargaining, once positions are stated, commitments made, and options narrowed, the negotiators are arguing about what they will or won't do. The subject of the discussion is the unwillingness of each negotiator to do what the other is asking. In crude form, it may be a shopkeeper saying, "I won't sell that secondhand bike for less than $75," to a potential buyer who is saying, "I won't pay more than $45 for it." From there on, the dialogue is likely to be focused on some form of pressure to get the other negotiator to do what he just said he wouldn't do. "You'd better sell it now or you will have to carry it over the winter." "If you want a bike for this weekend, you'll have to buy this one. There are no other shops open Friday evening."

These tactics are inherently coercive because they focus on the other person's will power, not his reason. When we use them, we are not reasonably addressing the issue between us — the price of the bike — but trying to undermine the other's will and ability to refuse our demand.

Try to persuade them of what's fair. In focusing a negotiation on statements of what they will or won't do, negotiators often avoid discussing what they *should* do. They fail to discuss external criteria that might serve as appropriate benchmarks for deciding the matter fairly. Legitimacy in the eyes of both is one measure of a good outcome. And it is often easier to give in to an external standard than to an arbitrary position insisted upon by the other side. I feel coerced if I give in simply because you are prepared to be more stubborn than I am. I feel persuaded if you convince me by external standards that I am paying a fair price. "As a dealer, I paid $50 for this bike last week. Unless I make a 50 percent markup on secondhand bikes, I can't afford to carry them. Or look at it this way. It will cost you $25 to rent a bike over the weekend, so you would be paying only a weekend's rental plus what the bike cost me."

Worsen their walk-away alternative vs. Improve ours

Worsening their walk-away alternative threatens them. The most coercive tactic of all is to threaten bad consequences to those on the other side if they do not agree with us. Rather than focusing on creating an agreement that will satisfy their interests as well as ours, we focus on convincing them that if they don't agree with us, we will hurt them.

In a one-on-one negotiation, I might say, "If you don't give me the raise I want, I will quit and write a letter to all your customers giving them good reasons why they should take their business elsewhere."

Threats focus on the consequences of failing to agree. A useful acronym for these consequences is BATNA — the Best Alternative To a Negotiated Agreement.* When I threaten you, I am saying that your BATNA is worse than you may think, because I am going to make it worse. If my threat produces agreement, it is because you have been coerced. You are agreeing not because agreement is attractive, but because nonagreement has become less attractive.

When I make a threat, there are three possible outcomes: I "win" the encounter because you back down; you don't give in, so I carry out the threat; or you don't give in, and I decide not to carry out the threat. None of these outcomes is good for the relationship. None will make it easier for us to deal with differences in the future. All point toward problems "next time."

Improve our walk-away alternative. Much of my negotiating power depends on what I can do if we don't reach agreement. In some situations, I can make you more willing to agree with me by improving my alternative of dealing elsewhere — by strengthening my BATNA. If you are asking $75 for a bike, I may be able to find a friend who will sell me his bike, which is slightly better, for $60. Unless you come down to $55, I will buy my friend's bike for $60. In this circumstance, I have not worsened your BATNA but have bettered mine. I am not threatening to hurt you. Rather, I am honestly disclosing that unless we can reach

---

*Suggested in *Getting to YES*, Chapter 6. Both the concept and the acronym have been accepted in the literature. See, for example, Howard Raiffa, *The Art and Science of Negotiation* (Cambridge, Mass.: Harvard University Press, 1982).

agreement within a certain range, it will be to my interest to walk away. You may feel constrained by the situation, but not illegitimately coerced. My conduct need not damage our ability to deal well with differences in the future.

While coercive tactics will in almost every case damage a working relationship, alternative persuasive techniques are consistent with each of the other elements in this book. Persuasive modes of influence are unconditionally constructive for our relationship — they will be more likely to produce better outcomes for me and to improve our ability to work together in the future, whether or not you use them too.

9 | Acceptance

Deal seriously with those with whom we differ

NO AMOUNT of rational thinking, clear understanding, accurate communication, trustworthy behavior, or persuasive influence will build a working relationship if each side rejects the other as unworthy of dialogue. A relationship may be brief or ongoing. It may be one from which either side can walk away at little cost. Or, like a relationship between parents or between the United States and the Soviet Union, it may be unavoidable. If you and I are going to deal well with our differences, I will have to accept our relationship as a fact and accept you as someone with whom to deal — as someone whose interests and views are worth taking into account.

Rejection creates physical obstacles to problem-solving

At its simplest level, the rejection of someone with whom I have conflicting interests physically prevents communication. I slam the door. I walk away. I hang up the telephone. I refuse to negotiate. I condemn myself to deal with a situation without the information you could provide and without an opportunity to inform or persuade you. We are in a situation together, but I pretend that we are not.

149

For forty years, Palestinians and Israelis have been rejecting each other. Sometimes Palestinian leaders, sometimes Israeli leaders, and sometimes both at the same time have been telling each other that they are not acceptable people with whom to negotiate. This rejection has created practical obstacles to the kind of communication and understanding that would help them deal with their important differences.

Rejection creates psychological obstacles

Even where rejection creates no physical impediment to communication — where the people involved remain physically able to talk and listen to each other — rejection may create psychological barriers that are equally obstructive. If I insist that I am better than you or reject your views as worthless, I may undermine your desire to work with me. This is true even in a brief encounter. Consider the following example:

Driving on a narrow country road through woods, I come slowly around a curve and collide, head on, with an automobile being driven by a young woman, apparently in her teens. We are both shaken up but appear unharmed. The cars, however, have significant damage: smashed headlights, broken front grilles, and crushed or dented fenders.

One approach to the relationship in this situation is to question the competence of the other driver, to blame her for the accident, and to deny the legitimacy of her story. Such a rejection makes it difficult to deal with the problem the accident created. As an example of that kind of rejection, consider the following dialogue:

Statements	Effect
"What the hell were you doing driving like that?"	Cast blame.
"Typical woman driver."	Belittle the other. Categorize in negative stereotype.
"There's no excuse for that kind of driving. Don't try to make one up."	Reject the worth of the other driver's views.
"Who's responsible for you? Is this your father's car? Where can I reach him?"	Look for someone of more "value" to talk to.

After such an exchange, the other driver is likely to feel unheard, belittled, and angry. These reactions will reduce the likelihood:

- that she will try to communicate effectively with me;
- that I will come to understand her perception of the situation;
- that either of us will come to trust the other; and
- that either of us will persuade the other.

There is little chance that we will work well together.

Rejection can be damaging even if it isn't total. At some point in our lives, each of us has been "put down" by someone else. A law professor may ask, "And if you were going to *think* before you answered that question, what would you say?" A headwaiter may simply look down his nose. In every profession, nationality, and organization, there are people who try to increase their importance by putting down someone else.

In the business and bureaucratic world, the use of jargon

and the dropping of names — however intended — is often received as an exclusionary message: "I am in the inner circle; you have not been admitted." Titles, private dining rooms, special security clearances, and other perquisites of office are sometimes used in a way that makes us feel that in the eyes of the other, we are less than equal.

With governments and political organizations, nonacceptance may create both psychological and physical barriers. The impact on Israelis of being told that Jews do not belong in the Middle East — and the impact on Palestinian Arabs of being told that they do not have a right to self-determination — limits both communication and a desire for greater understanding of the other.

In South Africa, blacks hear the message that they are inferior, not accepted as equal negotiating partners. This is the same message Americans hear when they are called "capitalist imperialists" — and no doubt the message that Soviets hear when their country is called an "evil empire."

In personal, business, and governmental relationships, nonacceptance, whether express or implied, sends the message that I am right and you are wrong, that I have nothing to learn from you, and that you have little value. Receiving that message is likely to reduce any interest you might otherwise have in communicating with me, in understanding how I see things, in trusting me, or in working with me. In effect, I have announced that I have made up my mind about you, that you don't matter to me, and that I will not be influenced by anything you say. There are few more powerful ways for me to sabotage our ability to deal with differences.

Accept unconditionally

With some people, such as a panhandler on the street, I may rationally decide that I don't want a relationship and may deliver that message by acting in a way that rejects him. But if I do want a working relationship with you, I will have to accept you as someone with whom to work. It makes no sense to reject a relationship with you if my goal is to deal well with our differences.

As Chapter 3 points out, if we are going to deal well with disagreements and problems between us, then my ability and willingness to deal with you must continue in spite of those disagreements. If I need to resolve differences that involve both of us, I need to deal with you. I do *not* need to approve of your behavior. We will be better able to accept a relationship if we clearly distinguish acceptance and approval.

We often express strong disapproval of another's conduct by refusing to deal with them. Finding someone's *conduct* objectionable, we conclude that the *person* is unworthy of our time and effort: "After what she did, I will never talk to her again." "Since we disapprove of what the African National Congress is doing, we will not meet with them." Favoring a relationship with someone whose conduct we do not favor may strike us, and our constituents, as inconsistent. It seems easier and clearer to reject both the person and his behavior. No one can claim that I approve the conduct of my good-for-nothing son if I cut him off and refuse to talk to him. But my action will just as clearly destroy any ability to work out our differences.

The Bible tells us, "Love thine enemy," but does not suggest that we should approve of his conduct. We should care, show concern, be willing to listen, and be willing to work with him in a problem-solving relationship. We need not turn a blind eye to his bad behavior. But no matter how strongly we disapprove of his behavior, we need not dismiss him as worthless. If we want to deal well with our differences, we should not treat *him* as contemptible or swat him like a mosquito. A graphic paraphrase of the biblical injunction might be, "Do not kill thine enemy lightly."

If a boy skips school, his father is likely to disapprove. He might react in one of two ways. Fearing that any softness could be a signal of approval, he might close his mind to his son and say, "I don't want to hear any excuses. No son of mine is a truant." The son will feel that his father doesn't understand him, won't listen to him, and doesn't trust him. Father and son may be on the road to an ongoing history of unresolved disputes.

On the other hand, the father might respond, "John, I skipped a few classes in my time and learned to regret it. If you think you had a good reason for doing so, I want to hear it. But I want you to know that I don't approve of such behavior." John's working relationship with his father is likely to be good. The son will feel care and respect. But he will know that his father does not approve of cutting class.

We may find the concept of acceptance more palatable if we clearly understand that in accepting others for the purpose of a working relationship:

- we need not accept their values;
- we need not accept their perceptions as correct; and
- we need not approve of their conduct or consider it "acceptable."

What we *do* need is a willingness to deal with the *real* person, a willingness to hear his views and to accord his interests due process.

Deal with respect. All of us, in one way or another, stereotype. When we do, we are dealing with an image in our minds more than an individual before us. If we want to improve a working relationship, we need to respect the individuality of the real person.

Look behind the stereotype. We organize ideas in mental

images and theories that help us interpret events and behavior. To some extent, however, this leads us to see what we expect to see and to interpret what we see according to our assumptions and understanding. Categorizing information in this way simplifies our view of the world and helps us act with confidence. But we may also ignore new ideas and behave in ways that damage our ability to work with others. When we are firmly committed to a belief, and when new information is ambiguous, foreign, or apparently threatening, we are especially likely to interpret the new data, and the people involved, in accordance with some preexisting image.

It is essential to categorize and generalize. We cannot analyze every bit of information about everyone. But our tendency to prejudge can damage or preclude a working relationship when it determines whether, or how, we interact with others. And it becomes irrational when we interpret the same data in different ways according to our preconceptions. In one experiment, psychologists asked subjects to evaluate pictures of women according to their beauty, character, and whether the subjects would like them. Other subjects were asked to evaluate the same pictures, but with Irish, Italian, or Jewish names attached. The evaluations from the latter group conformed to ethnic stereotypes, whereas those from the former group did not.

We evaluate the behavior of foreign governments in a similarly distorted way. In October 1987, the U.S. government published a report asserting that the Soviet Union was using trade shows for U.S. businesses to gather "industrial intelligence," implicitly condemning the Soviets for this behavior. But anyone who has participated in a trade show knows that all U.S. businesses use them for a similar purpose, to find out what everyone else in the industry is doing. An image of the Soviet Union as a spying adversary — which is sometimes correct — leads the U.S. government to interpret all Soviet behavior as evil, even when that behavior is accepted business practice among U.S. companies.

We tend to form the most prejudicial images of groups that are clearly different from us and that may pose a threat to our political, social, or economic structure. These images become rooted in our emotions and are often difficult to change. Marxists, blacks, Shiites, and Jews are all victims of such prejudice.

We tend to denigrate those whom we prejudge. We are likely to discount them, their views, and their interests. When we close our minds to their views, they are likely to close their minds to ours and ignore our interests. We may then see their behavior as confirming our image and discount their interests still more. We become even less likely to believe that they are worthy of our concern and attention. In these circumstances, we will find it difficult to work out our differences.

Deal with the real people. To overcome a stereotype I may have about you, I will need to know more about you. One way for me to break out of a stereotype is to focus on the particular history of the individual person with whom I am now dealing. If I am dealing with the woman in the accident, for example, I can seek to learn as much as possible about the events in her life. Where is she from? What family does she have? What does she care about?

Even if I am dealing with an institution about which I may have some stereotype, I can improve my ability to handle differences if I focus on individuals. A "radical" union or "union-busting" management becomes something I can deal with when the cardboard characters in my mind are replaced by a few real people, with names, faces, homes, children, jobs, and hobbies. If we can step outside our institutional roles and interact at a personal level — have lunch or visit one another at home — we will almost certainly shatter some preexisting generalizations. And we will find it more difficult to dismiss each other as unworthy.

It is important for me to become aware of how much I am unconsciously stereotyping. Before entering a meeting or negotiation with someone quite different from myself, I might jot down what facts I really know about him, question my assumptions, and plan to get to know him personally.

Give their interests the weight they deserve. If I expect to reconcile my interests with yours and work out my differences with you, I must recognize your interests and take them into account. Even if I believe you are unreasonable or evil, I need to accept that you have *some* legitimate interests. Many instances of violence in the world today have been motivated by the failure of one ruling or powerful group to respond to the interests of another, perhaps less powerful group. Once a government judges an opposition group as unworthy of respect, the government often ignores its interests altogether. This is often true even though an objective observer, using the government's own standards of fairness as a rule, would judge some of the weaker group's interests legitimate. In South Africa, for example, the whites have rejected the right of full democracy and equality for the blacks, a right they steadfastly defend as legitimate for themselves. Similarly in Israel, the government has failed to advance any plan that would accommodate the interests of the Palestinians in free elections and self-government, even though the Israelis would consider these rights essential for themselves.

They are equally entitled to have interests. Just as we are entitled to our own opinions, so we are entitled to our own interests. We may dislike the interests of strip mining companies, oppose the interests of conservative political action committees, or fear the interests of the Soviet Union, but we should respect their right to *have* interests. Unless we do, we will not be able to deal with them. And if we do not, we are likely to promote anger, rebellion, and unilateral actions that will damage our own interests.

Apply due process. One social mechanism for solving problems in the United States revolves around the courts. If we have been wronged and our interests damaged, we can take our case to a judge. The courts provide a forum where the interests of even the most meek are accorded due process, and they resolve conflicting interests within the bounds of the law.

Equally important from a social point of view is a fair way of dealing with *nonlegal* interests. Without a mechanism to take differing human, social, and political interests into account in a way that appears legitimate, the social fabric of a society — its ongoing relationships — may tear. And any one relationship is likely to tear if the interests of one side are regularly ignored. Listening is not enough. The competing interests need to be balanced in a way that appears legitimate, and interests accorded the weight they deserve.

This does not mean that we must adopt an amoral philosophical stance, that there is no right or wrong. I can and should make a judgment about the weight to be accorded your interests. But if you and I are to deal well with our conflicting interests, my judgment needs to be made on the merits after I have given your views a fair hearing.

Treat them as equals — in basic respects. Implicit in many working relationships is the idea that each party accepts the other as an equal partner. If I believe, however, that I have a high status justified by seniority, skill, or knowledge, I may be reluctant to accept you for fear of giving up that status. I may be afraid that my acceptance of you may go to your head and that you may assume that you now deserve a greatly expanded role in our decision-making.

We need not ignore differences. The owner of a large ranch told the story of his generally incompetent ranch-hand who, nonetheless, was an excellent carpenter. He asked the hand to build a gate and volunteered to serve as helper on the job in order to get it done quickly. The job was well done, and the owner commended the hand for it. The next day the hand quit. He said that if he was smart enough to boss the owner, he was too good to be working as a hired hand.

A boss who treats her secretary as an equal in one respect may find the secretary behaving as an equal in every respect, including taking long lunch hours. I would like to have a cordial and effective relationship with my plumber, my doctor's receptionist, and my young student, but perhaps not to the extent that they feel free to drop in and make themselves at home. A boss who treats all employees as equals may find that some want an equal say on questions properly within the boss's jurisdiction. The very step that one takes to make it easier to deal with differences may thus enlarge them.

There are many well-functioning relationships, such as parent-child, supervisor-employee, and faculty-student, that do not involve equality. In Japan, as in some other cultures, a large part of the social structure rests on concepts of hierarchy based on seniority or status. That hierarchy does not seem to interfere with the problem-solving approach for which the Japanese are well known.

Presume equality unless objective merits warrant differences. A good working relationship need not require us to eliminate an inequality based on skill or seniority. Expertise, experience, or authority should get its due — no more and no less. In general, if two unequal partners in a relationship might accept as reasonable the same inequality between two other people, then that inequality seems justifiable. For example, we would probably all accept the superior judgment of a doctor on a medical problem or the superior authority of a judge to decide a lawsuit. We want good working relationships between people with different skills and with different degrees of authority. And those with more skill or authority need not give up their status in order to work out differences with others of less skill or authority. Yet there is no reason to defer to a doctor in matters of politics nor to let a judge overrule the views of the rest of the family on what television set to buy.

When we accept someone else as an "equal" negotiating partner, we want to convey an acceptance that is broad enough to promote rationality, understanding, communication, reliability, and the use of reasoned persuasion rather than coercion, but we also want to express that acceptance in a way that manages expectations. A "working" acceptance need not be so broad that it purports to eliminate justifiable differences between us. Common sense and our own experience suggest that each partner should accept the other as equally human, equally caught up in the situation, equally entitled to have rights, and equally entitled to have any interests and views taken into account. How we do this will depend on the person and the circumstances, but the presumption of equality should guide us.

But, what if . . . Many of us may be reluctant to accept another person, especially when we have strong differences with them, because we believe that acceptance will damage our interests or weaken our position relative to them. Some of these assumptions, such as a belief that acceptance will require us to approve of their conduct or give up some justifiable advantage, are tied to mistaken assumptions about what kind of acceptance we need for a good working relationship. Other fears, however, may be the result of faulty assumptions about the consequences of acceptance. Any of these assumptions might lead me to bar a relationship with you. But I may find that rather than protecting me, my barriers weaken my ability to deal with my fears.

Fear: Won't acceptance encourage bad behavior? If I have had a policy of not dealing with you because of our differences, it is likely that you have been doing things I disapprove of. As the head of a radical student organization, you may have been conducting disruptive demonstrations. As a member of a Basque separatist organization, you may represent people who are engaging in illegal violence for political purposes. At this point, my recognizing you, accepting you as a negotiating partner, does two conflicting things.

Beneficially, it opens the door for greater consultation, greater understanding, better joint problem-solving, and nonviolent means of influence. But also, and perhaps costly from my point of view, it appears to reward your illegal violence and encourage more. Since you wanted some kind of recognition, committed acts of violence, and then got recognition, there is a danger that the very act of opening the door to nonviolent negotiations will encourage more violence. If I want to turn a bad relationship into a more constructive one and accept you as a negotiation partner, I will have to do so in a way that limits both your expectations and the expectations of others.

Accept as a matter of policy. Acceptance as a matter of routine confers no special status. Each year, the control of dozens of governments around the world changes, some by democratic vote, others by armed struggle. If the U.S. government regularly refused to recognize those new leaders it disapproved of, it would weaken its ability to influence events around the globe. To avoid this, the government follows a standard policy (with a few notable and costly exceptions) of recognizing all governments that have de facto control of their countries. Because this is standard policy, a regime of which the United States disapproves, such as the current government of Afghanistan or Nicaragua, can claim no special status or success from the fact that the United States maintains diplomatic relations with it.

It is true that if in the past I have refused to meet or talk with you, then changing my policy and granting you a new "accepted" status may cause problems. You may believe that I have given in to your pressure and may apply more pressure to gain some substantive concession. I may have raised your expectations. The mistake, however, lies not in my later act of acceptance, but in my original refusal to deal with people who are important to me. We can avoid such problems in the future by adopting a policy of accepting, listening, and dealing with anyone in whose behavior we have an interest.

Since only discretionary acceptance conveys any special significance, adopting a nondiscretionary policy of acceptance should manage expectations and avoid the appearance of rewarding bad behavior. If our policy is universal, even if it is a change from the past, our willingness to deal with a particular adversary is neither a concession nor sign of weakness. And rather than rewarding bad behavior, our openness will help us deal with it.

Fear: Won't supping with the devil contaminate me? I may fear that if I associate with "bad" people, some of the dirt will rub off. My feelings about you may run so deep that I cannot bring myself to deal with you. I may believe that if I accept you as someone whose interests deserve to be taken into account, I will lower myself to your ethical level, however low that may be. I may further worry that sitting down with a bitter adversary will contaminate my image in the eyes of my constituents.

At a governmental level, castigating a foreign foe is frequently a good way to divert attention from domestic problems and gain popular support. To change the tune, however — to tell one's public that yesterday's "imperialist aggressors" are now those whom we want to engage in joint problem-solving — is likely to involve domestic political costs. A leader will be reluctant to change quickly from open hostility to open acceptance. The fact that many of the public may confuse our "acceptance" of another government with "approval" of its conduct will further increase the perceived cost.

Many think that if the United States had a good working relationship with Castro, it would be better able to influence Cuba and Latin America. But having made isolation of Castro a publicly supported policy for so long, even a new administration may find it politically costly to establish relations. Fear of constituent doubts may be especially strong if a leader believes there is a significant risk of failure. Some believe that General Secretary Gorbachev may pull back from his plan to build relations with the West if the effort does not begin to show tangible results for Soviet constituents. A more conservative course, although less likely to improve relations and reach satisfactory substantive results, is likely to be less risky in the short run.

By supping with the devil, we learn more ways to deal with him. Whatever our reasons for identifying the other side as the devil, the devil we know is easier to handle than the devil we don't. Removing impediments to communication and understanding better equips us to deal with reality. No matter how bitter a divorcing couple may feel toward each other, they are more likely to keep their assets out of the pockets of their lawyers if they can negotiate an agreement rather than battle in court.

A political or union leader who has rallied support around a policy of rejection will, it is true, face short-term political costs if he changes his policy. But he will be better able to produce substantive results for his constituents by dealing with the other side. Similarly, only by accepting Israel and dealing with it was President Anwar Sadat able to negotiate the return to Egypt of the entire Sinai Peninsula. A leader will want to focus the eyes of his constituents as much as possible on the long-term benefits of the new policy.

Fear: Won't I give up a bargaining chip? I may believe that since you want my respect, care, and acceptance, I ought to get something for it; to give it away for nothing weakens my bargaining position.

The United States has said that it might talk with the Palestine Liberation Organization if the PLO first committed itself to the unconditional acceptance of Israel's right to exist. Here, the withholding of acceptance of the PLO is apparently being pursued as a bargaining tactic. The United States is negotiating about negotiating, in the hope that at a distance it can influence the PLO more effectively than it could in a better working relationship. But not talking with the PLO makes it extremely difficult to work out a formula that might be acceptable to both the PLO and the United States. No one can be sure that such a formula exists, but the possibility of devising one would certainly be greater if the United States were talking with Palestinian representatives rather than insisting, without any dialogue, on particular phraseology formulated by the United States.

Accepting you allows me to bargain more effectively. Withholding acceptance as a strategy to gain a concession is like negotiating by telephone and, as a tactic to persuade you, yanking the telephone out of the wall. It may be dramatic, but it is unlikely to get me anything in return and it handicaps me for the future.

For years, the PLO crippled itself by withholding acceptance of Israel as a "trump card" with the hope of getting something for it later. But bargaining over acceptance is like bargaining over an apology. The longer it is held back, the less valuable it becomes. Like an apology, acceptance is constructive when given, not when withheld. Trying to use acceptance as a bargaining chip is coercive. It creates distrust and precludes the inventing of options that will best accommodate conflicting interests. Perhaps most important, it is likely to establish an adversarial pattern of behavior that will damage the way people deal with each other long into the future.

My influence will be more powerful if I deal with you rather than try to ignore you. The differences between Japanese and U.S. labor relations may again illustrate the point. When unions began to organize in this country, management generally refused to accept or deal with them. Through the end of the nineteenth and the first half of the twentieth century, this refusal led to increasingly adversarial relations between management and workers. This relationship persists, and it has damaged U.S. competitiveness to the detriment of both management and labor.

In Japan, on the other hand, management began at an earlier stage of the labor movement to accept the role of workers in corporate decision-making. As a result, labor and management have worked together to improve quality and efficiency, and both have benefited from the surge in Japanese exports.

Behave as if we care — and we will

Even if I try to modify my behavior to show acceptance, to overcome stereotypes, to weigh your interests, and to show you equal respect, will this really make a difference? Won't you be able to see through my performance? If I believe that I am superior, won't you hear rejection in the tone of my voice, see it in my eyes, and feel it in every move I make? Can acceptance be insincere and still effective? And if in my heart I truly reject you as an inferior, as someone I despise and whose interests I would like to ignore, what do I do?

The concern is well deserved. Caring about the other person provides a strong motivation for making a relationship work. We care about those with whom we share close relationships — families, friends, and allies. What happens to them matters to us. My concern for your present and future circumstances motivates me to solve problems jointly with you. My honest demonstration of that concern is likely to encourage you to solve problems jointly with me. And it would be unrealistic to expect me to feel the same level of concern for an adversary that I feel for a friend. How much caring is enough? And how do I generate it?

Some caring is essential for a good working relationship. If I treat you as an instrument, a means to serve some interest of mine and nothing more, you will have no incentive to work with me. Unless the relationship serves your ends as well as mine, it is not likely to serve either of us well. A relationship that is purely instrumental is not very instrumental. I have to care enough about your interests to motivate you to work with me. This level of caring is partly intellectual and partly emotional.

As a first step, I need to acknowledge intellectually some degree of interdependence. I need to accept the fact that we have shared or conflicting interests and that, to deal with them well, we will have to deal with them together. Under these circumstances, like it or not, we have a relationship. My ambivalence — knowing that I need to work with you, but not wanting a relationship of any kind — may make me behave in ways that upset you and prevent effective interaction.

From 1917 to 1933, for example, U.S. aversion to the Soviet system, and perhaps fear of it, led to continued rejection. Intellectually, our diplomats knew that we could not solve our problems with the Soviets unless we accepted them. But, as a country, we could not bring ourselves to do so. The United States as a whole had to overcome an intellectual and political threshold, to acknowledge to itself and to the Soviet Union that its security and well-being depend on its ability to deal with the Soviet government.

Once we intellectually accept that our relationship partner matters to us — that we cannot solve our problems alone — we can honestly behave in ways that will improve our joint ability to deal with differences. There will be no sham in our inquiry as to their perceptions and interests. We need to know them to advance our own interests.

Once I begin to pursue an effective relationship *with* you, I am likely to change the way I think *about* you. If I start treating you as a worthy individual, equally entitled to your opinions, I am likely to learn that there are areas where your knowledge and skill are superior to mine and that some of your opinions are clearly worthy of respect. If I try to understand how you see things, I am almost certain to learn that my own perceptions are more subject to bias than I had previously thought. If I behave as though I were more reliable, I am likely to become more conscious of my commitments and more committed to them. If I listen more actively and behave as if I were open to persuasion, I may find, to my surprise, that I am persuaded more often than I would have expected. If I treat you as someone who matters, you will begin to matter to me.

Changing the way we behave changes the way we think.

Applying the theory to practice

How might these ideas apply to a particular case and help me begin a relationship constructively? Let's return to the collision between my car and that driven by a young woman. I would like my opening words to help set a tone that will allow us to work out our problems. Our relationship may not be long-term, but so long as we deal with each other I want it to work.

Instead of confrontation:	**Try an "acceptance" approach:**
Stereotyping: *"Woman driver."*	Focus on the individual: *"What's your name?"*
	Elicit her story: *"Tell me what happened from your point of view."*
Belittling the other: *"That was a stupid thing to do."*	Show concern and respect: *"Are you hurt?"*
Rejecting the legitimacy of the other's views: *"I don't want to hear your excuses."*	Be open and seek understanding: *"I think I understand how you could see it that way."*
Rejecting the worth of the other: *"Who's responsible for you?"*	Ask advice: *"What do you think we should do now?"*

I will never know what I might learn unless I open the door. In this case, it is just possible that the young woman is a wealthy doctor who was rushing to take care of a patient; she is terribly sorry about the accident, believes it was her fault, and was going to propose that she pay for the repairs to both cars — until my hostile approach made her angry.

Acceptance is not just something that happens. Nor is it something that is relevant only the first time you meet. Forming a relationship is not adopting a resolution, where we can draft appropriate language, vote on it, and then all but forget it. A relationship is more like a garden: it is constantly changing. It needs regular attention or it will go to seed. Demonstrating acceptance of the other is both an initial act and a continuing requirement. Each time an incident in a relationship comes up, it provides an occasion for either judging and rejecting others or for demonstrating our interest in dealing with them as people who count. Dealing seriously with others helps us deal wisely with our differences.

III | The Elements as Parts of a Whole

10 Congruence

Put it all together so that it fits

A LOT — perhaps most — of this book is just organized common sense. Some of it, no doubt, rings true to your experience. Certainly you knew much of it already. Still, developing a relationship that deals well with differences is difficult. Personal, business, and above all international relationships need attention.

If much of what this book suggests is common sense, why do we still have relationships that don't work? Why is there a gap between apparent common sense and practice? One explanation may be that although we know many bits and pieces of advice that make sense, we do not put them together and apply them appropriately and consistently to produce a coherent and effective relationship.

The elements that affect the performance of a working relationship make up an interdependent system. A weakness in any single element damages the performance of the whole. Rational behavior and plenty of clear communication will not make a relationship work if misunderstanding, mistrust, coercive behavior, and expressions of rejection persist.

We often take individual actions that in themselves seem appropriate, but that taken together produce a strategy that

173

lacks coherence. Our actions will not yield an effective working relationship if they are inappropriate for the particular situation, discordant with each other, or inconsistent with what we think.

To build an effective working relationship, I will want to overcome these difficulties. I will want to combine the elements so that my actions are:

- congruent with the particular relationship and situation;
- congruent with each other; and
- congruent with my beliefs.*

Be congruent with the particular relationship and situation

So far, this book has been considering characteristics that are desirable for any kind of relationship, whether personal, business, or governmental. An underlying hypothesis has been that general theory will be more helpful and more powerful than ideas that apply in only one context. And it is usually easier to understand difficulties in a big international or business relationship when we see them in a personal relationship. In every kind of relationship it is helpful to understand the other's interests, to be reliable, and to communicate carefully. But applying such guidelines, no matter how valid, to a particular case requires care. Relationships do differ, and our efforts to improve one should take its special qualities into account.

Some of us tend to handle all interactions in a similar

---

*Although we may associate "congruent" with triangles in a geometry class, dictionary definitions support our three senses: "suited to the requirements of the case," "consistent," and "corresponding in character." An 1878 usage is apt: "Each new conclusion has to be . . . dove-tailed into the rest, made congruent with the system of thought" (*Oxford English Dictionary*).

way. We develop habits that we follow no matter with whom we are talking. We may deal with people in a manner we learned from our parents. For instance, every time we get into an argument with a family member, we may leave the room or go out for a walk. We may find that something works in one encounter and use it with others. And as we grow older, we may grow more rigid.

A uniform approach will produce some good relationships but also some bad ones. Some people need more listening and understanding, others more acceptance and caring; others need security, and still others will bristle at even a hint of coercion. We cannot hope to behave in the same way with all people and produce a good working relationship with everyone.

Consider what is special about the other side. In general, I want to tailor my behavior to fit a relationship with a particular person — you. And no matter how rational, understanding, listening, reliable, open, and accepting I *think* I am, it is your needs, your perceptions, and your opinions that count.

I need to understand what makes you different and unique. If, for example, you are the kind of person who wants a high degree of predictability, I should find ways to be extremely reliable. If you are a loan officer at a bank where my company has an ongoing relationship, I should try to learn, not only about you, but also something about the demands you face in your job and the decision-making procedures of your bank.

Dimensions along which relationships are likely to differ include:

Emotion. Some people tend to be far more emotional than others. They may express their feelings more freely and be more affected by them. I may not be able to synchronize my emotions with yours, but I should at least be aware of the differences. If I approach a problem with cool, detached logic while you approach it with feeling, I may cause more problems than I solve. I should try to anticipate the emotional level of an encounter and adjust my approach accordingly.

Expectations. Your expectations will affect your reactions. To be effective in dealing with you, I will want to know all your expectations: about relationships, about what is likely to happen, about me, and so forth. I may not want to conform to those expectations, but knowing them will make it easier to avoid unnecessary conflict.

Pace. A major cross-cultural difference in the way people approach problems is the speed at which they act and expect others to act. Americans, particularly in an East Coast business environment, often move at a hectic pace; appointments and travel plans are tightly scheduled. Among other peoples and in other parts of the world, life proceeds more leisurely. An awareness of the speed at which my partner normally functions can greatly facilitate our ability to work together.

What is and isn't done. Every culture — and every family — develops patterns of conduct that govern, not only people's expectations, but how comfortable they are with others' behavior. Some things are done; some things are not done. It is often difficult for those who have grown up with a certain pattern of behavior to articulate the rules. Becoming aware of our own "rules of the game" and discovering our partner's is not easy — and is sometimes painful. A newly married wife may be jolted and upset to learn that her husband, instead of waiting until Christmas morning, opened her present to him on Christmas Eve! When such trivial do's and don'ts can cause problems, we can appreciate the importance of discovering our partner's assumptions in more significant areas. If we don't know each other's rules, we are likely to bungle our problem-solving.

Formality; reserve. A particular norm of behavior is likely to guide the formality with which people operate. People from Israel and from the western part of the United States are likely to be particularly informal. They may start right off on a first-name basis, dress informally, and drop in unexpectedly. In many other parts of the world — for example, in Tokyo and London — greater formality is the norm. And formality tends to correspond with reserve, greater respect for privacy, and greater social distance in personal matters.

In seeking to make my actions appropriate to a situation, I will want to recognize such variable qualities in my relationship partner.

Evaluate the state of the relationship. Before setting out to improve a working relationship, we may want to assess the present situation. This may be particularly true when a relationship is well established, whether it is personal, as with a spouse, or institutional, as between two governments. Ongoing relationships often become set in their ways and need a fresh look.

Checking a relationship from time to time can help prevent serious difficulties from arising. Too often with a relationship, as with our health, we assume everything is fine until something goes wrong. Just as visiting a doctor for a regular checkup can help maintain the health of our bodies, so an occasional reflective "checkup" can help maintain the well-being of an important relationship. It can be useful to think in general terms about the implicit goal of a relationship and the strategy for reaching that goal. Reviewing each element — with the relationship partner, if possible — we can identify areas that require attention. Sitting side by side, recalling recent encounters, and listing specific questions for discussion can stimulate fresh ideas for improving our pattern of interaction. Just as a doctor might use a checklist in reviewing our physical health, I might use a checklist along the following lines to see how well a relationship is going:

How Good Is Our Relationship?

A CHECKLIST

GOAL
Am I trying to win the relationship or improve it?
How well do we resolve differences?
How often do I think about improving the process for
  working together over the long term?

GENERAL STRATEGY
Do serious substantive issues disrupt our ability to work
  together?
Do I tend to retaliate by doing things that weaken our ability to deal with each other in the future?
Do I ignore problems or sweep them under the rug rather
  than deal with them?

Balance of EMOTION and RATIONALITY
Awareness: What emotions, mine and yours, are affecting
  our interactions?
Effect: How are emotions helping and hurting our
  decision-making?

Degree of UNDERSTANDING
How well do I empathetically understand your: percep-
  tions? interests? values? motivation?
How well can I state them to your satisfaction?
How well do you understand mine?
Can you state them to my satisfaction?

How effective is our two-way COMMUNICATION?
  How regularly do I consult you before making decisions?
  What important subjects don't we discuss? Why?
  How extensively and frequently do we communicate? Do I
    listen?

**RELIABILITY: How much confidence do you have in my
future conduct?**
  Might I be more reliable? How?
  How could I be more worthy of trust?
  Do your perceptions suggest some changes I might make?
  What risks do I see in relying on you? Are those risks well
    founded?

PERSUASION or COERCION
  Do I try to persuade you on the merits?
  Could I be more open to persuasion? How?
  How well do I avoid threats, warnings, and commitment
    tactics?

Degree of mutual ACCEPTANCE
  Do I fully accept you as someone with whom to deal?
  Do you matter in my scheme of things?
  Am I giving serious attention to your interests and views?
  Do I recognize the potential long-term quality of this
    relationship?

  With practice, we will quickly recognize problems in a
working relationship, deal with them day to day, and dis-
pense with a checklist. But it is useful to stop from time to
time, consider each element in a relationship, and think
about how it might work better.
  Although much of the advice in this book is common
sense, all of us are occasionally guilty of senseless behavior. A review of our important relationships may indicate

areas of weakness. This is certainly true of the U.S.-Soviet relationship, in which each government regularly behaves in a way that we would not normally find sensible.

The December 1987 summit meeting in Washington, D.C., between President Reagan and General Secretary Gorbachev provided a useful opportunity to reflect on the historical relationship and the immediate potential for change. In going through a full evaluation of the relationship, a few points stand out.

Goal. Many officials in each government focus on changing the substantive policies of the other government, and they measure the success of the relationship by that standard. Many considered the Reykjavik summit in 1986 to be a failure because the two sides failed to reach agreement. And even at the December 1987 summit, a Soviet Foreign Ministry spokesman indicated that he would consider the summit a success only "if we prepare ground" for "the second treaty on strategic arms" (*New York Times,* December 8, 1987, p. A14). But the leaders also indicated in Washington a view for the long-term working relationship. President Reagan said, "We can only hope that this history-making agreement will not be an end in itself, but the beginning of a working relationship that will enable us to tackle other issues, urgent issues, before us" (*Washington Post,* December 9, 1987, p. A28).

Strategy. Both the U.S. and Soviet governments tend to mix substantive issues with relationship issues and play one off against the other. Historically, the relationship has deteriorated when disputes have become serious. The "spirit of Camp David" created at the summit between President Dwight Eisenhower and General Secretary Nikita Khrushchev in 1959 disintegrated when the Soviets shot down a U-2 spy plane over Soviet territory. Similarly, the détente of the 1970s crumbled when it was unable to handle disputes over emigration, trade restrictions, and military support for insurgencies in Angola and elsewhere. In 1980, President Jimmy Carter withdrew the U.S. team from the Moscow Olympics in retaliation for the Soviet invasion of Afghanistan. While some might have considered this a substantive reciprocal action, it damaged efforts to improve understanding and predictability between the two countries. More recently, the United States has tended to link its willingness to deal with the Soviets to human rights policies. The U.S. delegate to the Helsinki Accords review conference in May 1985 said, for example, "Performance in the field of human rights is inextricably linked to all aspects of improved bilateral relations" (*New York Times,* May 16, 1985, p. A14). And President Reagan said just before the Reykjavik summit, "I will make it clear to Mr. Gorbachev that unless there is real Soviet movement on human rights, we will not have the kind of political atmosphere necessary to make lasting progress on other issues" (*New York Times,* October 8, 1986, p. A6).

A few months earlier, the Soviets responded to the U.S. bombing of Libya in April 1986 by canceling a meeting between Foreign Minister Eduard Shevardnadze and Secretary of State George Shultz which was to have laid the groundwork for the Reykjavik talks. "The Soviet leadership has warned that such actions cannot but affect relations between the USSR and the United States. Unfortunately, this warning was not heeded in Washington. In effect, the Administration itself has made impossible at this stage the planned meeting on the level of the foreign ministers" (*New York Times,* April 16, 1986, p. A19).

At the December 1987 summit, the leaders gave hopeful signals that they would try to work together despite and because of serious substantive differences. President Reagan remarked that "while we have fundamental disagreements about how human communities should govern themselves, it's possible all the same for us to work together." And General Secretary Gorbachev said, "Without minimizing the great political and ideological distances between us, we want to seek and find avenues of rapprochement in areas where this is of vital importance for our two countries and for all humankind" (*Washington Post*, December 9, 1987, p. A29).

Emotion. The relationship between the Soviet Union and the United States has long been affected by strong feelings of fear and suspicion. General Secretary Gorbachev acknowledged this at the December 1987 summit when he said that any rapprochement between the two countries must struggle against "long-held emotions and stereotypes" (*New York Times*, December 9, 1987, p. A20). The Washington summit engendered helpful emotions of enthusiasm. Emotions became so strong in favor of cooperation, however, that there was a real risk of overwhelming reason with euphoria. An administration official noted that the atmosphere was so positive that "the biggest problem is to keep the enthusiasm down" (*Washington Post*, December 9, 1987, p. A24).

Understanding. Neither the United States nor the Soviet Union understands the other well. On the particular issue of the U.S. Strategic Defense Initiative (the so-called Star Wars program), for example, each government appears to be locked into positions without understanding the interests of the other. The United States acknowledged in 1985 that Soviet work on defensive weapons "might open the door to a potential first strike" (*New York Times*, March 20, 1985, p. A19), but the United States does not acknowledge that the Soviets might have similar concerns about U.S. defensive weapons. Similarly, the Soviets do not appear to understand the U.S. view that defensive weapons hold out the real possibility, under some circumstances, for increasing military stability.

Communication. Both governments confuse their communications by talking to multiple audiences. Each uses public statements to communicate with its own people, its allies, and its bureaucracy as well as with each other. After the Reykjavik summit, the Reagan administration sent confusing signals to the Soviets when it interpreted the events of the summit in a way intended to placate conservatives in the United States. General Secretary Gorbachev responded, "Besides distorting the entire picture of the Reykjavik negotiations, the United States took actions in the last few days that look simply wild in the normal human view after such an important meeting. . . . What kind of government is that, what can one expect from it in other affairs in the international arena? To what limits does the unpredictability of its actions go?" (*New York Times,* October 23, 1986, p. A12).

The Soviets have created equal problems with lack of candor and clarity in their communication. This was particularly evident in the aftermath of the Chernobyl nuclear accident, when Western countries could not get accurate information about it.

Trust. Each government harbors a strong suspicion of the intentions and conduct of the other. But each government focuses on the violations of the other rather than on what it can do to improve reliability in the relationship. The United States is suspicious of the Soviet Union in part because Soviet conduct in the past has been aggressive and unreliable. But the reaction of the Reagan administration often made matters worse. In 1985, Secretary of Defense Caspar Weinberger and Director of the Central Intelligence Agency William Casey advocated, eventually successfully, renouncing the SALT II treaty. They explained their argument by saying that "renunciation is the only way to show that the United States is serious about compliance" (*New York Times,* May 31, 1985, p. A3). Such an argument is confusing at best.

Both President Reagan and General Secretary Gorbachev expressed their desire for increased trust at the Washington summit talks, but neither focused on what he could do by himself to improve reliability and accurate risk assessment in the relationship. Either leader could start by improving the reliability of his own conduct, taking even minor promises seriously, and carefully assessing, without exaggeration or derogation, the risks of relying on the other's commitments.

Coercion. Each government regularly tries to coerce the other into adopting different policies. The Soviet government tries to coerce the United States into abandoning aid for the contras in Nicaragua, while the United States tries to coerce the Soviets into changing their human rights policies and withdrawing from Afghanistan.

Public opinion is a common lever for coercing the other. A U.S. administration official at the arms talks in Geneva commented in 1985, "This is going to be fought out in Western newspapers and legislative bodies. It will not be settled by the force of logic and reason in Geneva" (*New York Times,* March 21, 1985, p. A10). Former President Richard Nixon recognized the coercive effect of this public diplomacy, and its unproductive result, with regard to human rights: "We should make human rights a top-priority private issue, but not a public issue. . . . The more public pressure we placed on Soviet leaders, the more intransigent they would become" (*Christian Science Monitor,* October 31, 1985, p. 12).

It is unclear in 1988 whether the superpower leaders accept the need for persuasion rather than coercion as the primary mode of influence. President Reagan, at the fare-well ceremony of the December 1987 summit, noted only, "We've proven that adversaries, even with the most basic philosophical differences, can talk candidly and respect-fully with one another and with perseverance find common ground" (*New York Times,* December 11, 1987, p. A22).

Acceptance. The governments of the United States and the Soviet Union have each treated the other with disdain and rejection at one time or another. In 1982, President Reagan referred to the Soviet government as an "evil em-pire," and Soviet leaders have called the United States an "imperialist oppressor." The epithets reflect strongly felt emotions of rejection. Both governments have been quick to judge the moral character of the other. In 1986, President Reagan reasserted his desire to "publicly define the crucial moral distinctions" between the two countries (*New York Times,* October 7, 1986, p. A4). And the Soviets, pointing to homelessness, poverty, and drug addiction, have fre-quently derided the moral faults of capitalism and Western society. Such judgments have been anything but construc-tive, making each side less willing to deal with the other.

The Washington summit, however, introduced a tone of acceptance. General Secretary Gorbachev noted, "We know what our interests are, but we seek to accommodate them to the interests of others, and we are ready to meet each other halfway, as equals" (*Washington Post,* Decem-ber 9, 1987, p. A29). President Reagan similarly expressed a desire to "work together" with the Soviet government.

If the United States and the Soviet Union were to review their working relationship regularly, they might focus more attention on showing acceptance, behaving reliably, trying to understand the other, and clarifying signals. It would help remind both governments that for many reasons they have a shared interest in improving the way they deal with their differences and that doing so is a shared task. A better working relationship could save each country from economic strain. And it could save the world from the worst possible consequences of a bad relationship.

Pay more attention to the more important relationships. Sometimes the effort required to understand the other party in a relationship, to evaluate the current state of each element in the relationship, and to shape our actions so that they are fully appropriate to the time, place, and people involved will be more than it is worth. My working relationship with the corner grocer is not worth the attention that is due my relationship with my daughter-in-law or my spouse. The U.S. government's relations with Albania are not worth the attention due its relations with the Soviet Union. While reviewing a relationship, we should evaluate its importance and allocate our attention accordingly.

Make our actions congruent with each other

The elements of a working relationship work together. We often focus on only one or two elements and frequently notice only faults in another's behavior. A man ending a relationship with a woman might say, "I thought we had a great relationship because we could talk about anything. But I felt manipulated — she would always try to get me to do things her way." The woman might have a different view: "Yes, we could talk about anything, but he made me feel as though my opinions weren't worth much." These two might have been able to improve their relationship if they had gone beyond communication to work together on other elements, starting with acceptance and understanding.

A failure of any one element can damage the effectiveness of a relationship. If I were to meet someone from a different culture — an Afghan or a Japanese, for example — I might accept him as someone worth dealing with and make an effort to be rational, communicative, trustworthy, and open to persuasion. Yet if I failed to understand how he saw things, it is unlikely that we could work well together.

It is not too hard to make my actions internally consistent when all of them are directed toward the single goal of improving our working relationship. Harmony among the various things I do is more difficult when — as is almost always the case — some of my actions are taken in pursuit of an immediate goal. I am likely to be inconsistent. I may act one way on one day and, because the facts are different or because I am under more stress, act quite differently another day. I may deal differently with different people. You may observe the inconsistencies and question my sincerity.

Our ability to deal well with differences will be strengthened to the extent that all our efforts reinforce each other. There is a natural harmony among the different aspects of the guidelines developed in this book. Imagine the notes that a wife might make as she reexamines difficulties that have come up in her marriage and suggests to herself what she might do about them. The checklist on the next two pages illustrates the way the elements work together.

In preparing a list like this, the elements can serve as a checklist, but it quickly becomes clear that the suggested approach toward a working relationship is not a list of disjointed actions. If Bob's wife were to pursue such a program, he would not feel seven different strands separately. The success of the approach would depend upon its becoming a coherent whole, each aspect in harmony with the others.

NOTES TO MYSELF

about how I can help Bob and myself deal with disagreements

Emotions

If I am getting upset, let him know. (Communicate.)

Maybe take a break. (But consult before deciding.)

Maybe give him a hug or a kiss. (Words are not the only way to send a message.)

Understanding

Whenever I'm confused, uncertain, or uncomfortable about why he is doing something, be curious.

Find some time every day and have the courage to try to get him talking about what's on his mind.

Put myself in his shoes. Try to look at a problem the way it must look to him.

Communication

Get Bob's input before making any big decision (or even a small one) that affects him.

Ask his advice on anything that's worrying me.

When he's talking, LISTEN.

Evaluate his views without judging *him*.

Reliability

Consult him before making commitments.

Consult before changing my mind or changing plans.

Try to be on time. (If I can't be, let him know.)

If his plans change, don't score points. Be understanding. Suggest ways for him to let me know about such changes in the future.

Persuasion	Be open. Listen. Try ideas on for size; they may fit.
	Avoid pressure tactics.
	Don't escalate an issue; pursue each issue on its own merits.
	Face our differences side by side; put the problem on the wall.
	Generate a lot of ideas; look for good ideas, not just mine or his.
Acceptance	Take his interests and ideas seriously; I'm not always right.
	Go over this list with Bob and get his suggestions.

Use the same guidelines even if the relationship is brief. We often act inconsistently with a good working relationship when we assume the relationship will be short. But however short a relationship (and it often continues beyond original expectations), its ability to function well will depend upon the same basic qualities of understanding, good communication, reliability, and so forth, that we have been discussing.

We can avoid inconsistencies that undercut the effectiveness of a relationship by acting as though every relationship were going to be long-term. This does not mean that we should devote the same resources and effort to a short-term relationship as to a long-term one, but we should use the same guidelines. Even in negotiating with the repairman at an out-of-town garage, we should be rational, understanding, communicative, reliable, and nonthreatening. We should accept him as somebody with interests and views

Be Congruent: Use Each Element So That

	Acceptance: **Deal with them seriously despite all differences**	**Rely on *Persuasion*, not coercion**
Rationality: **Balance emotion with reason**	Don't just think about them — care; they matter.	Use emotion to persuade, not to coerce.
Understanding: **Learn how they see things**	Understand their views before judging them.	Understand them in order to persuade them more easily.
Communication: **Always Consult Before Deciding**	Speak with them, not about them.	Acknowledge good points. Speak for ourselves; don't put words into their mouths.
Reliability: **Be wholly trustworthy, not wholly trusting**	Deal with them to reduce the risks.	Avoid overstatement and deception.
Rely on *Persuasion*, not coercion	Respect their right to differ. Take them seriously.	

that deserve to be taken into account. Those guidelines will help this interaction whether or not we ever see him again. And we may.

Although this book looks separately at each element of a good working relationship, and at a strategy for building it that is unconditionally constructive, every element affects every other. The table above illustrates just one way in which every guideline informs and supports every other.

It Is in Harmony with Every Other

Reliability: **Be wholly trustworthy, not wholly trusting**	*Communication:* **Always Consult Before Deciding**	*Understanding:* **Learn how they see things**
Don't let emotions make us unpredictable.	Acknowledge feelings. Be aware of theirs.	Understand empathetically.
Assess the actual risks of trusting them.	Consult. Inquire. Listen actively.	
Be honest. Disclose areas we are not discussing.		

Revise our behavior and beliefs until they are congruent

We are not going to build a sound working relationship if we simply wear a new approach like a new suit of clothes, trying to cover up beliefs and values that are quite different. One businessman, when asked at the end of a seminar to write down a lesson he had learned, wrote:

Be "SINCERE."

Discussion confirmed that for him "sincerity" was an

impression to be created in the minds of others. But he did not yet see it as true consistency between his conduct and his beliefs. His goal, rather, was a mask that would make him *look* sincere.

Any approach to building a good working relationship is likely to fail if it clashes with your own beliefs and values. Each aspect of your behavior will be more effective if it rings true, and it is more likely to ring true if it *is* true. If the guidelines are uncomfortable, if they don't fit your working assumptions, reexamine both the guidelines and your assumptions. Pretending to be honest is not the same as being honest. If the way you are trying to behave is not in harmony with the way you are thinking and feeling, it will be difficult to establish the kind of relationship that allows you to work well with others.

The ideas suggested here are not notes for someone you should pretend to be. A lot of ideas have been advanced. Try some of them on for size. You may discover that they fit, and that the you inside those ideas is not exactly the person you thought you were.

No single plan for building a good working relationship will work for everybody. Adopt one that fits your personality. If you are quiet and reserved, don't try to improve communication by wearing the face of a noisy extrovert. Find quiet times to talk. Noting how others behave may help you broaden your repertoire, but to be effective you don't need to imitate others or pretend to be someone you are not. Never abandon the power of saying what you believe and believing what you say.

Joint work on a relationship helps bring things together

This book has focused on what each person in a relationship can do to improve their joint ability to deal with differ-

ences. The emphasis on our own actions has been deliberate, because it is so easy in a relationship to blame the other
side. Each of us, all by ourselves, can do an enormous
amount to improve the quality of a working relationship.
The other party holds no veto over *our* constructive action,
and we can further our interests without waiting for
reciprocity.

One of the most constructive activities, however, is to
talk with a relationship partner about what it means to have
a good working relationship and about ways to get there.
You might start, for example, by asking someone you deal
with to read and mark up this book as a basis for discussion.
Or you might hand over a checklist or notes you prepared
along the lines of those in this chapter, and suggest that you
jointly prepare ones relevant to your situation. Particularly
for relationships in the labor, business, and governmental
areas, joint workshops, seminars, and informal discussions
that cover some of the issues raised in this book are good
ways to initiate joint concern with how differences are
being handled.

Discussing honestly our joint ability to deal with differences is almost certain to reduce misunderstanding, improve communication, and convey the message that each of
us accepts the other as someone with a contribution to
make in dealing with joint problems. A good working relationship will work even better when we work on it together.

A Note on
"Tit-for-Tat"

Analytical
Table of Contents

Table of Charts

A Note on
the Harvard
Negotiation
Project

A Note on "Tit-for-Tat"

Some game theorists suggest that in a bilateral relationship the best strategy is a reciprocal one known as tit-for-tat: after the first interaction, I do to you whatever you did to me the last time. In many cases, it is not clear whether this advice is meant to apply to relationship issues as well as to substantive offers and demands. Since this book reaches the conclusion that the best guideline for building and maintaining a good working relationship is to act in various ways that are unconditional — ways that do not reciprocate what another does — it seems worthwhile to add a note reconciling our conclusion with those who favor tit-for-tat.

Game theorists have compared the dynamics of bilateral relationships with a model known as the Prisoners' Dilemma. In one anecdotal illustration of this model, two men suspected of committing a major crime are confined separately. The prosecutor is certain that they are guilty but lacks enough evidence to convict them. He tells each suspect that he has a simple choice: confess or not confess. If the prisoners cooperate with each other and neither confesses, each can expect a one-year sentence for illegal possession of a weapon. If both confess, each will get an eight-year prison sentence for the major crime. If one confesses and the other does not, the one who refused to confess can expect a ten-year sentence, but the one who confessed will get lenient treatment for turning state's evidence and can expect to get off with simple probation. The prisoners cannot communicate with each other.

Each prisoner now faces a dilemma: "If the other is going to confess, I'd better do so too, because eight years is better than ten. If the other is not going to confess, I'd better confess, because then I will get off lightly. It thus seems to be better to confess no matter what the other does. But if we both confess, we are both worse off than if we both refuse to do so."*

This model also fits many common situations. Suppose you and I are trying to decide whether to buy Christmas presents for each other. I can buy shirts (which I know you want) at a discount, and you can buy socks (which you know I want) at a discount. Each of us must decide without knowing what the other is going to decide. How generous should each of us be in buying a present and mailing it off to the other? If both of us are generous, we come off well. But in the short run, at least, if you are stingy, I am better off being stingy. And if you are generous, I am still better off being stingy. So it looks better for me to be stingy no matter what you do. And the logic works the same for you. And yet, if we are both stingy, neither of us gets the benefit of the discounts. Hence the dilemma.

The following chart illustrates the choices in a Prisoners' Dilemma situation. The individual decisions are indicated by either C (cooperate: be generous) or D (defect: be stingy).

---

*This is an edited version of the account given in Duncan R. Luce and Howard Raiffa, *Games and Decisions* (New York: John Wiley, 1957), p. 95.

	YOUR BEHAVIOR	
	Cooperate	Defect
MY BEHAVIOR		
Cooperate	(CC) I win You win	(CD) I lose big You win big
Defect	(DC) I win big You lose big	(DD) I lose You lose

If the game is to be played over and over, computer simulations suggest that the best strategy to adopt without knowing the other person's strategy (the strategy that yields the most value after many iterations) is cooperative tit-for-tat; that is, cooperate and be "generous" the first time, and thereafter do whatever the other side did on the previous exchange.

Within the constraints of the model, tit-for-tat may well be the best strategy. With regard to some substantive issues, Prisoners' Dilemma may be an apt model and tit-for-tat a reasonable strategy. As we have noted, reciprocity is an appropriate measure of fairness in substantive negotiations.

Some people infer from this that tit-for-tat is a reasonable strategy for relationship-building, particularly in foreign relations. Robert Axelrod, in *The Evolution of Cooperation* (New York: Basic Books, 1984), notes that tit-for-tat "might also be useful in promoting cooperation in international politics." Yes and no. On some substantive matters, a good way to negotiate may be to act first and call for reciprocation. Charles Osgood's "GRIT" proposal (*Gradu-ated Reciprocation in Tension-Reduction* [Urbana: Univer-sity of Illinois Press, 1961]) was based on this theory. But as a strategy for building a working relationship — for im-proving the way we deal with differences — tit-for-tat would be a mistake. This is true for two reasons:

1. With regard to relationship issues, a bilateral relation-ship is *not* a Prisoners' Dilemma. In the Prisoners' Di-lemma, I make myself worse off by being generous if you are stingy. But with regard to understanding, for example, if I try to understand you, I am better off regardless of whether you try to understand me. The more I understand you, the better I will be able to anticipate your actions even if they are malicious. This is true for each of the relation-ship elements discussed in detail in Chapters 4 through 9. I am better off pursuing a better relationship, regardless of whether you follow suit. (See the following chart.)

	YOUR BEHAVIOR	
	Cooperate (Try to understand)	**Defect** (Do not try)
MY BEHAVIOR		
Cooperate (Try to understand)	(CC) We both under-stand each other well.	(CD) I understand you well, but you don't understand me.
Defect (Do not try)	(DC) I don't understand you, but you un-derstand me well.	(DD) Neither under-stands the other. We continue to do poorly on problem-solving.

Although this chart focuses on the element of under-standing, the relative payoffs are the same with regard to any of the elements of a working relationship. The relative outcomes are clearly different from those in the Prisoners' Dilemma scenario. Each of us can be sure that we are better off if we pursue cooperation on the relationship issues, re-gardless of how the other responds. There is no dilemma.

2. Since relationship issues do not fit the Prisoners' Di-lemma model, the analysis suggesting tit-for-tat does not apply. Furthermore, trying to pursue tit-for-tat on relation-ship issues may be dangerous.

If we follow a tit-for-tat strategy, partisan perceptions are likely to lead to malignant spirals in our relationships. In substantive areas, it may be relatively easy to estimate the value of the other side's injury or concession to us. We can evaluate their move and reciprocate. This is certainly true in the model of the Prisoners' Dilemma, where there are only two possible choices. But in the real world, and with relationship issues in particular, we tend to see the other's actions through our own bias, and we are likely to interpret their behavior as worse than ours.

If I pursue a policy of tit-for-tat, partisan bias will tend to cause me to evaluate your behavior as worse than mine and reciprocate with behavior that is equal in my eyes, but worse in yours. Since you are likely to interpret mine as being worse than I thought or intended, you will reciprocate with behavior that is even worse than your initial behavior. Since our assessment of the qualities of a working relation-ship — levels of emotion, understanding, communication, reliability, acceptance, and noncoercive behavior — is likely to be highly subjective, a policy of tit-for-tat will lead to ever-worsening behavior. This is especially true in ad-versarial relationships, where partisan bias is especially

strong. In those relationships, a tit-for-tat strategy on relationship behavior could easily lead to a downward spiral of
substantive actions and reactions as well.

Examples of the downward spiral that can result from tit-
for-tat strategies in international relations are common.
When the United States decided to expel Soviet United Nations diplomats in 1986, the Soviet Union reciprocated. The
U.S. retaliated by expelling more diplomats, and the Soviet
Union responded by withdrawing all Soviet support staff
from the U.S. Embassy in Moscow. This deterioration almost derailed the Reykjavik summit, which was scheduled
for later that year, and may have contributed to the mixed
results of that meeting.

Tit-for-tat may make sense on some substantive issues.
Perhaps it is a good policy for me to give you a present this
Christmas as fine as the one you gave me last year. But on
the qualities identified as crucial to joint problem-solving
there is no dilemma; I can pursue an unconditional strategy
without risk. If you are acting in ways that injure your own
competence, there is no reason for me to do the same. Two
heads are better than one, but one is better than none.

Analytical
Table of Contents

INTRODUCTION

I. *An Overview*

Chapter 1: THE GOAL
A relationship that can deal well with differences

II. *Basic Elements of a Working Relationship*

Chapter 4: RATIONALITY
Balance emotions with reason

Chapter 5: UNDERSTANDING
Learn how they see things

Chapter 7: RELIABILITY
Be wholly trustworthy, but not wholly trusting

DEALING WITH OUR OWN RELIABILITY

DEALING WITH THEIR RELIABILITY

DEALING WITH SYSTEMS THAT
AFFECT RELIABILITY

Chapter 8: PERSUASION, NOT COERCION
Negotiate side by side

Chapter 9: ACCEPTANCE
Deal seriously with those with whom we differ

III. *The Elements as Parts of a Whole*

Chapter 10: CONGRUENCE
Put it all together so that it fits

Table of Charts

A Note on the Harvard Negotiation Project

The Harvard Negotiation Project is a research project at Harvard University which works on negotiation problems and develops and disseminates improved methods of negotiation and mediation. It is part of the Program on Negotiation, a consortium of scholars and projects from Harvard, MIT, Tufts, and elsewhere trying to improve the theory and practice of conflict resolution. The Project's activities include:

Theory building. The Project has helped develop such ideas as the one-text mediation procedure, which was used by the United States in the Middle East peace negotiations at Camp David in September 1978; the method of principled negotiation, summarized in *Getting to YES: Negotiating Agreement Without Giving In* (Houghton Mifflin, 1981), which has been translated into a dozen languages and sold more than a million copies; and the theory of unconditionally constructive relationship management, explained in this book.

Education and training. The Project develops programs for professionals (lawyers, business people, diplomats, journalists, government officials, union leaders, military officers, and others) and is working on courses for university and high school students. Each year, the Project offers two week-long courses to lawyers and the general public as part of Harvard Law School's Program of Instruction for Lawyers. Interested persons should contact the Program of Instruction for Lawyers, Harvard Law School, Cambridge, Massachusetts 02138; telephone: (617) 495-3187.

Publications. The Project prepares practical materials, such as *International Mediation: A Working Guide* (still in a draft edition), checklists for negotiators, case studies, and forms designed to be of use to practitioners, teachers, and students. Inquiries about teaching materials available for distribution should be directed to the Program on Negotiation Clearinghouse, Pound Hall 513, Harvard Law School, Cambridge, Massachusetts 02138; telephone: (617) 495-1684.

Action research. Participants in ongoing conflicts, international and domestic, are sometimes invited to the Project so that its members (and the participants themselves) may learn more about the negotiation process and so that participants may benefit from the ideas developed at the Project and other professional advice.

U.S.-Soviet collaboration. The Project has undertaken an ongoing relationship with colleagues in the Soviet Union to analyze and try to improve the way the superpowers resolve differences. This work, funded largely by the Carnegie Corporation of New York, includes research on current negotiation methods, joint articles published in the United States and the Soviet Union, and an ongoing effort to affect constructively the superpower negotiation process.